W9-BTP-884

MASTER BUILDERS

A GUIDE TO FAMOUS AMERICAN ARCHITECTS

Building Watchers Series

EDITED BY DIANE MADDEX

PRESERVATION PRESS

John Wiley & Sons, Inc.
New York   Chichester   Brisbane   Toronto   Singapore

Printed in the United States of America
10 9 8 7 6

Library of Congress Cataloging in Publication Data

Master Builders.
   (Building watchers series)
   Bibliography: p.
   Includes index.
   1. Architects—United States—Addresses, essays, lectures.   I. Maddex, Diane.   II. National Trust for Historic Preservation in the United States.
III. Series.
NA736.M37   1985   720'.92'2 [B]   85-16982
ISBN 0-471-14402-9

"Cram and Goodhue," by Richard Oliver, is adapted from his book, *Bertram Grosvenor Goodhue* (The Architectural History Foundation and The MIT Press, 1983). Copyright © 1983 by the Architectural History Foundation and The Massachusetts Institute of Technology. Reprinted by permission of the MIT Press.

Back cover quotation from Vincent Scully, *American Architecture and Urbanism* Frederick A. Praeger Publishers, 1969). Copyright © 1969 by Vincent Scully.

Designed by Anne Masters.
Edited by Gretchen Smith. Composed in Trump Medieval by Carver Photocomposition, Inc., Arlington, Va., and printed by BookCrafters, Inc., Fredericksburg, Va.

Contents

Introduction

If you have just acquired this book, you are probably familiar with a few of the 40 architects and their works discussed in the following essays. But you are the exception. Most people know precious little about architecture and architects. Not many people ever require architectural services or can count an architect among their acquaintances.

Why should you want to know more about these architects? The reason is simple. You are undeniably connected to the built environment that you inhabit, use, see and respond to. You affect building design, and building design affects you. Therefore, it seems of more than passing interest to know something about the architects whom society charges with the complex task of creating buildings and cities.

The public knows little about how architects work or why they design as they do. For many, the image of the architect is fashioned by occasional, popularized heroes found in literature, films and television—Howard Ruark in Ayn Rand's *The Fountainhead*, forever locked in our movie memories by Gary Cooper's stoic screen portrayal, or Paul Newman doing it his way in the *Towering Inferno*.

Very few architects become public celebrities. Those who become famous usually do so when their design achievements or design influence attract the continuing attention of colleagues, critics, historians and the media. Discussion and publication of their buildings, design awards and newsworthy revelations about their personalities can bring national and international stature.

Fame can be elusive and fleeting, of course. An architect could spend a lifetime designing many very good buildings that are functional, safe, economical and attractive, buildings that are waterproof, structurally sound, comfortable, easy to maintain and efficient to operate. Yet, fame may never come to such an architect, despite satisfied clients, good social connections and a remunerative practice.

Detail of *The Architect's Dream*, by
Thomas Cole, 1840, which depicts
the architect contemplating
idealized forms of the architectural
tradition. (Toledo Museum of Art)

On the other hand, an architect whose buildings may be technologically, functionally and
economically lacking but are judged to be visually exciting and artistically innovative may well
achieve worldwide fame. Why?

Our culture and those who analyze and record
it ultimately place greatest value on that which
transcends service or functional performance.
Great architecture has always represented more
than responsible construction or durable shelter.
Artfulness of form and artistry of building have
long been the dominant standards for measuring
the extent to which human-made artifacts are
transformed from the profane to the sacred.

It is easy to take architects and architecture
for granted. Environmental form, purpose, patterns of space and volume and surface, decorative elements and systems of support and climate control confront you every day. You look at
them without truly seeing them. But architects
want you to be moved by what you see, to be inspired, to experience buildings and spaces profoundly through your senses and intellect. Architecture can become symbolic as well as
beautiful, paradigmatic as well as practical.

Aesthetic standards and judgments are historically relative, however, influenced by temporal
circumstances and trends. Scholars constantly
reexamine the past and reconsider their prede-
cessors' evaluations, sometimes reaffirming
them, sometimes contradicting them. Such cycles of review used to be lengthy, gauged by centuries or, at the most frequent, generations. To-

day the cycles of reconsideration and revision-
ism are much shorter, measured in years. Thus,
a current list of the most famous might be
viewed differently in five or 10 years.

Who is on this book's current list? Among the
most famous and influential are Thomas Jefferson, Frank Lloyd Wright, Ludwig Mies van der
Rohe, Walter Gropius and I. M. Pei. All of these
men and their best works are known throughout
the world. Charles Bulfinch, Benjamin Latrobe,
Frederick Law Olmsted, H. H. Richardson,
McKim, Mead and White, Adler and Sullivan,
Richard Neutra and Skidmore, Owings and Merrill are included and familiar.

But you may be uncertain about William
Strickland, John Haviland, Richard Upjohn, Orson Fowler, Irving Gill or Addison Mizner, sim-
ply because their works and personalities have
been less well publicized than others on the list.
Note too that only one woman, Julia Morgan, is
featured (and a second, Denise Scott Brown, is
included with her firm); this situation is likely
to change in coming decades as more women become architects. And many on the list were born
in Europe, although all practiced in the United
States.

These 18th-, 19th- and 20th-century architects may not be universally considered the
"best" American designers. But most architects
and architectural scholars would probably agree
that they are indeed among the most "famous"
and that their fame is likely to be enduring. In
some way, they were all exceptional.

It seems to me that there are two kinds of famous architects. One kind, the rarest, invents new architectural visions, new forms, new aesthetic languages and vocabularies. Such architects are "form-givers," originators of unprecedented styles. The other kind is more evolutionary, adapting and refining preexisting architectural forms and styles in unique and often sophisticated ways.

The great modern "form-givers" in this book include Gropius (more as a teacher than a designer), Mies van der Rohe, Wright and Kahn. They influenced Neutra, Saarinen, Johnson and Pei, who in turn created their own unique, sometimes mutable styles. Think of post–World War II corporate office buildings, and you have to think of Skidmore, Owings and Merrill, legatees of orthodox modernism until recently. Venturi is a special kind of inventor, not of a singular style but of a philosophy of design advocating "complexity and contradiction" over simplicity and forced unity. He is thought by many to be the midwife of Post-Modernism and the return to historicism in architecture.

Before the mid-20th century, when much of the innovative, antihistoricist architectural thinking of European modernism and the International Style arrived and took hold in America, mainstream architects continued to pursue an architecture based on revival or adaptation of ancient classical, medieval or Renaissance images.

From 1890 to 1930, most significant public and private buildings in the United States were fashioned in the Beaux-Arts style. Hunt, McKim, Mead and White, Gilbert, Cram and Goodhue, Burnham and Root and many others designed buildings whose overall form and decorative motifs were transplants of historical precedents from Italy, Spain, France or England. Roman and Greek antiquity, rediscovered and transformed by the Renaissance, was considered the ideal source for architectural inspiration.

H. H. Richardson was able to synthesize a new style from an old one, the round-arched and turreted Romanesque, giving rise to a particular idiom unique to America. His work, along with that of Louis Sullivan and the Chicago School (the advent of the modern frame high-rise building), punctuated the end of the lengthy 19th-century Victorian era, when romantic theories about nature and building induced Gothic revivals and rejection of academic classicism. Architects Upjohn, Walter, Davis, Renwick and Mullett worked during this eclectic period, although the Beaux-Arts period that followed was equally eclectic.

American architecture at the end of the 18th and beginning of the 19th centuries went from the minimally decorated, relatively unpretentious Federal and Georgian styles derived from England to the intellectual rigor and formality of the first American classical revival of the early 1800s, evidenced by the works of Thornton, Bulfinch, Latrobe, Jefferson and Mills.

Again, while these men were highly original designers, they nevertheless confined themselves to the use of well-known classical vocabularies—column orders, arches, domes, pediments, decorative trim and plan configurations—that depended on legible, visual connections to monumental historical precedents in western European architecture.

Master builders present and past are unquestionably people of great creative talent and dedication. But most had other things going for them, significant determinants of an architect's fate. Many were highly educated and cultured, well read and well traveled, and no small number were born into families of wealth and influence. Like it or not, good social, business and political connections were (and remain) indispensable to developing prestigious practices and clienteles.

Some of these architects were iconoclasts, defying established conventions, norms of behavior or stylistic trends. Wright is undoubtedly the most famous such architect, now almost legendary as the design genius who arrogantly refused to conform, condemning all who questioned his beliefs or his work. As influential as Wright's design philosophy may have been, his egocentricity may have been even more influential.

Today's architect is much more likely to be working as part of a large, corporate team comprising many experts. The "prima donna" designer may be obliged to share authorship with several other decision makers. Nevertheless, because architecture remains an art, talented architects will always aspire to achieve a large measure of personal expression in their work. Fame, rather than fortune, could be one of their rewards. And some years hence, they too may be included in a book about master builders.

Roger K. Lewis

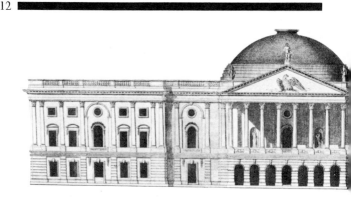

WILLIAM THORNTON
C. M. Harris

William Thornton (1759–1828) was born on a sugar plantation on Tortola, in the British Virgin Islands, but grew up among his Quaker relations in Lancashire, England. Although a young gentleman of fortune, he was apprenticed to an apothecary and then studied medicine at the University of Edinburgh, receiving the M.D. degree in 1784. He continued his studies in London and Paris and traveled in Europe and Scotland before coming to the United States in 1786.

Thornton established a medical practice in Philadelphia but found the fees small and the nature of physicians' work there "laborious" and "disgusting." His scientific accomplishments, however, gained him election to the American Philosophical Society, and his visionary turn of mind attracted him to the cause against slavery and to prospects for John Fitch's steamboat, to which he contributed designs as well as financial support. His "long attention to drawing and painting" and inclination for design led him to submit competition drawings for Library Hall for the Library Company of Philadelphia; his entry was selected in 1789. In 1790 he sailed for Tortola with his young bride, Anna Maria Brodeau, hoping to restore his dwindling fortune with a lucrative medical practice.

On Tortola he learned of the competition for the public buildings in Washington, D.C., and began a design for the proposed U.S. Capitol, which he carried with him on his return to Philadelphia in October 1792. After gaining additional information about requirements and site, he modified his initial plan (calling for a 500-foot front) and submitted drawings that, on the enthusiastic recommendations of Secretary of State Thomas Jefferson and President George Washington, were awarded the premium. While Library Hall exhibited features characteristic of British Palladianism, Thornton's Capitol was inspired more by the French tradition, particularly the east front of the Louvre (1667–70) and its 18th-century heritage.

Thornton served on the three-member Board of Commissioners of the Federal District from 1794 to 1802 and in that capacity exercised some sway over the execution of the Capitol and other public works. Although generally accepting of changes in the Capitol proposed by Jefferson or dictated by circumstances, he clashed sharply with superintending architects George Hadfield and Benjamin H. Latrobe when they sought to depart substantially from the basic design. Latrobe's

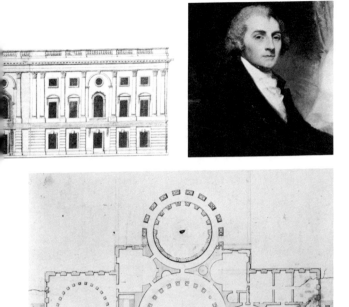

Right, top: William Thornton, by Gilbert Stuart, 1804. (Mellon Collection, National Gallery of Art)

Opposite and above: U.S. Capitol, engraving of the East Front from Thornton's drawing of his modified competition design, c. 1795, and the working plan, c. 1794, incorporating a "grand conference room" with a colonnaded loggia in the West Front (later eliminated). (Conrad Schwarz, Library of Congress)

alterations of the interiors eventually prevailed, but the configuration and, more important, the conception of the Capitol remain Thornton's enduring contribution and legacy.

In 1802 President Jefferson appointed Thornton superintendent of the Patent Office, a position he held (and needed for income) until his death. Although government service proved demanding and a wide range of interests absorbed him, Thornton produced innovative designs for two Washington, D.C., residences that exemplify the ideal of republican simplicity in the domestic architecture of the new nation: the John Tayloe III town house, known as The Octagon (1799–1802), and Thomas Peter's villa, Tudor Place, completed in 1816. One of two elevation drawings he prepared for the University of Virginia influenced Jefferson's design for Pavilion VII and his decision to employ rounded columns rather than square pilasters in the colonnade that unites the principal university buildings.

A serious and sophisticated, if, strictly speaking, amateur artist, Thornton is significant for his experimentation with the classical vocabulary and his efforts to express the meaning of the new American political order in architectural form. ◣

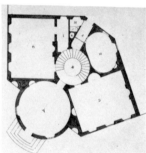

Library Hall (1789–90), Philadelphia. The directors of the Library Company slightly altered Thornton's competition design, since lost. (William Birch, Independence National Historical Park)

Preliminary plan, The Octagon (1799–1802), Washington, D.C., an innovative plan using a circle segment to position the house on a 70-degree odd-angle corner lot. (Library of Congress)

The Octagon, exhibiting the notable play of site and geometric form that distinguishes this design from other Federal-style houses. A hipped roof was added around 1818. (American Institute of Architects Foundation)

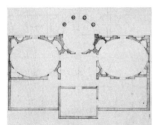

Preliminary plan and elevation, Tudor Place (1805–16), Washington, D.C. Thornton's initial villa concept was modified, but it retained the central "temple" as the unifying focal element. (Library of Congress; AIA Foundation)

Tudor Place as completed, showing the original stuccoed wall surfaces, later replaced. (Armistead Peter III, *Tudor Place*)

Proposed elevation for a pavilion at the University of Virginia, Charlottesville, from which Jefferson designed Pavilion VII (1817–21). (Alderman Library, University of Virginia)

BENJAMIN H. LATROBE
Paul F. Norton

The Greek style for public buildings and the Gothic style for domestic buildings were introduced to America by Benjamin Henry Latrobe (1764–1820). Although not the first professional architect in America, Latrobe was the first to make a strong impression on the public, and his numerous pupils, particularly William Strickland and Robert Mills, extended his influence in the 19th century by continuing to design in the Greek Revival style. Latrobe's pupils aggressively advanced the status of architects in America so that by midcentury architecture was a fully recognized profession.

Latrobe was born at Fulneck near Leeds, England, where his father, a bishop of the Moravian Church, had become master of a Moravian school for young children; Latrobe's mother was American. Latrobe was sent to a Moravian school in Germany to prepare for the ministry, but, unsure of his personal qualifications, he suffered a breakdown there. In 1783 he returned to London.

Back in England Latrobe first attempted a literary career and published two historical books, but by nature he was a man of action. He became apprenticed to John Smeaton, a prominent civil engineer who built Eddystone Lighthouse, and then entered the architectural office of Samuel Pepys Cockerell in 1789, staying there until 1791. He quickly gained a thorough knowledge of architecture and decided to start his own office. The times were unfavorable because of England's sporadic hostilities with France in the 1790s, and Latrobe received commissions for only two houses and some renovations. Eventually his business went bankrupt. He decided to go to America and sailed in November 1795.

For two years Latrobe moved about Virginia, designing some houses, mapping a swamp, working on the Richmond Penitentiary (1797) and establishing important social and professional contacts. On a trip to Philadelphia he met Samuel M. Fox, president of the Bank of Pennsylvania. He moved to Philadelphia in 1798 after receiving the commission to design the Bank of Pennsyl-

Latrobe's preliminary perspective of the Bank of Pennsylvania (1798–1800), Philadelphia. (Maryland Historical Society)

vania (1798–1800), his most beautiful work. Its colonnades recalled the graceful Erechtheum in Athens; its proportions were as perfect as those of any ancient building. This was soon followed by other commissions such as the engineering feat of constructing Philadelphia's first waterworks (1800–02). He also designed several houses including Sedgeley (1799), built for William Crammond in the Gothic style.

For lack of appropriations, work on building the U.S. Capitol ceased in 1800, but when Jefferson became president he pressed for funds to complete the building. In 1803 he appointed Latrobe surveyor—i.e., architect—of the Capitol to oversee construction according to the plans of William Thornton. Much controversy ensued between Jefferson and Latrobe over Thornton's original plans, particularly for designing the interior. Compromises took place, and the south wing was completed. While the arches in the old Senate room of the north wing were under construction, one gave way, killing the clerk of the

Plan of Center Square engine, Philadelphia Waterworks (1800–02), drawn by Latrobe, reflecting his engineering skills and affinity for geometric shapes. (Stoudinger Collection, New Jersey Historical Society)

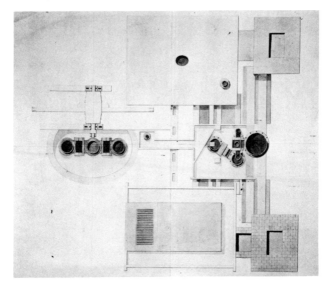

Benjamin H. Latrobe, by Charles Willson Peale, c. 1800. (White House Collection)

"Old West" (1803–04), Dickinson College, Carlisle, Pa., an example of Federal-style collegiate architecture. (Dickinson College)

Below and right: Latrobe's sketch of the U.S. Capitol (1793–1867), Washington, D.C., showing his unaccepted proposal for the central section. The corncob capitals in the Senate vestibule combine the classical and new American spirit. (Maryland Historical Society; Library of Congress)

works. People jealous of Latrobe's success and offended by his somewhat boasting manner never let him forget the tragic death and blamed him for it. Latrobe later furnished new designs for the Capitol after it was burned by the British in 1814 but resigned from his position in late 1817.

While working in Washington, D.C., Latrobe dominated its architectural style, designing, among other buildings, St. John's Church (1816) and Decatur House (1818–19). The Roman Catholic Cathedral (1805–21), Baltimore, designed without remuneration, stands today as his largest completed building. While in New Orleans in 1820 to assist his son, Henry, in building a waterworks, Latrobe caught malaria and died there.

The history of American architecture in the 19th century would undoubtedly have been very different if the French architects, such as Stephen Hallet, who worked at the Capitol, had introduced their version of classicism. But it was Latrobe's English background and firm intellectual and romantic leaning toward the ancient Greek style that pervaded the country, coming closer than any other to being the American national style. ◺

St. John's Church (1816), Washington, D.C., sketched by Latrobe. Originally a small square building, it has since been enlarged. (St. John's Church)

Decatur House (1818–19), Washington, D.C., detail of Latrobe's drawing of the hall. (Library of Congress)

Roman Catholic Cathedral (1805–21), Baltimore. The small cupolas were added later, replacing Latrobe's simpler domical tops. (Sandak)

CHARLES BULFINCH
Harold Kirker

Charles Bulfinch (1763–1844), America's first native-born architect, descended from a Boston family with an interest in building going back to the early 18th century. His architectural education began in the library of his Apthorp grandfather, a gifted amateur who was a friend and patron of the architect Peter Harrison, continued at Harvard College with studies in mathematics and perspective and culminated in a European tour planned in part by Thomas Jefferson. Significantly, what most impressed Bulfinch were Europe's recent rather than historic buildings. The work of Robert Adam and William Chambers in England and modern French planning for function and convenience provided the major inspiration for Bulfinch's American version of neoclassicism, first expressed in the Tontine Crescent (1793–94) and the Massachusetts State House (1795–97), both in Boston, and finally in the completion of the U.S. Capitol (1818–29), Washington, D.C., and the Maine State House (1829–32), Augusta.

The Tontine Crescent was the first important urban housing scheme undertaken in the United States, and the loss of his personal fortune in 1795 in attempting to complete it forced Bulfinch to accept permanent appointment as Boston's chairman of the board of selectmen and superintendent of police. In this unique position as architect-administrator, Bulfinch was in charge of the town's police, health, education, sanitation and poor residents. In addition, he also developed enormous commercial complexes, such as the India Wharf (1803–07) and Broad Street projects (1806–07), and designed scores of row houses, such as Park Row

Massachusetts State House (1795–97), Boston, its neo-Palladian character updated by neoclassical touches. (SPNEA)

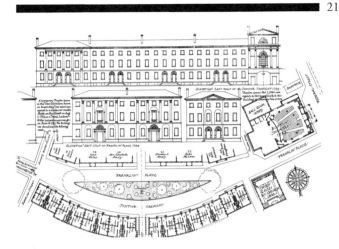

Tontine Crescent (1793–94), Boston, a single building with a central pavilion, encompassing 16 three-story brick townhouses. This building reflects Bulfinch's attempt to introduce monumental town planning to Boston. (Frank Chouteau Brown, Society for the Preservation of New England Antiquities)

Charles Bulfinch, by Mather Brown, 1786. (Harvard University Portrait Collection)

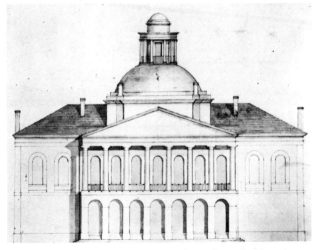

Maine State House (1829–32), Augusta, similar in plan to the Massachusetts State House but showing Bulfinch's growing interest in Greek Revival forms. (Maine Historic Preservation Commission)

India Wharf (1803–07), Boston, a commercial complex of more than a half mile of stores, warehouses and wharves. (SPNEA)

Third Harrison Gray Otis House (1805–08), Boston, with tall, triple-sash windows, typical of Bulfinch's style of domestic architecture. (SPNEA)

Church of Christ (1816), Lancaster, Mass., one of two surviving Bulfinch churches, complete with porch, portico, tower and cupola. (Samuel Chamberlain, Collection at the Essex Institute, Salem, Mass.)

(1803–05) and the Colonnade (1810–12), and free-standing mansions, such as the three Harrison Gray Otis houses (1795–96, 1800–02, 1805–08), and public buildings ranging from the State Prison (1804–05), Charlestown, to the Massachusetts General Hospital (1818–23), Boston. He leveled part of Beacon Hill, straightened streets, laid out parkways and malls and greatly extended the town's ancient boundaries. In the process Bulfinch created the most beautiful American city of its time and furnished the nation with an unrivaled model of urban modernity and efficiency. At the same time, his contributions to the commonwealth at large were hardly less notable, including University Hall (1813–14), Harvard University, Cambridge, and the Church of Christ (1816), Lancaster.

In 1817 President James Monroe visited Boston and was so favorably impressed by Bulfinch's professional skill, experience and adaptability that he appointed him architect of the Capitol. From the beginning of 1818 until

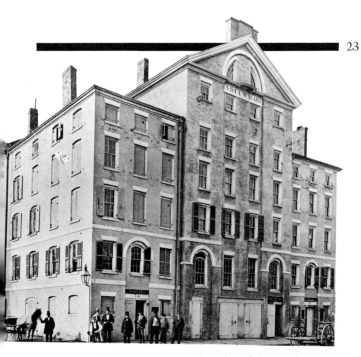

The Colonnade (1810–12), Boston, a row of 19 houses, part of Bulfinch's plan for the beautification of Common (Tremont) Street. (The Bostonian Society, Old State House)

Massachusetts General Hospital (1818–23), Boston, featuring characteristic Ionic columns, a giant portico and a stepped dome, rendered by Alexander Parris. The wings have been extended and the pediment altered. (Boston Atheneum)

the summer of 1830, Bulfinch resided in Washington, his major achievement being the completion of the Capitol after more than a quarter century of controversy. His direct contributions to this project were the western portico, the old Library of Congress, the original dome and the landscaping of the Capitol grounds. Before returning to Boston and retirement, he also designed the Federal Penitentiary (1827–28), Washington, D.C., and the Maine State House.

The formula for capitol buildings that Bulfinch developed over half a lifetime—the hemispherical dome and columnar frontispiece—decisively influenced the design of almost all subsequent state capitol construction in the United States in the 19th century. Thus, the regional style representing the federal ideal that Bulfinch initiated in Boston in the 18th century became the accepted architectural expression of American democracy in the 19th century.

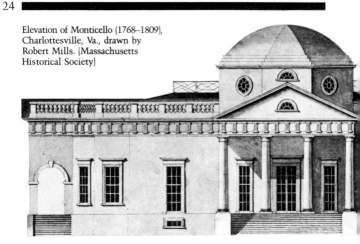

Elevation of Monticello (1768–1809),
Charlottesville, Va., drawn by
Robert Mills. (Massachusetts
Historical Society)

THOMAS JEFFERSON
William L. Beiswanger

Thomas Jefferson (1743–1826) was a self-taught architect
whose knowledge of the arts came from books and
observation. More than 700 of his drawings and notes on
architectural subjects have been identified, about half of
which relate to Monticello, his house near Charlottesville, Va. Begun in 1768, the design, construction and
remodeling of the house spanned more than 40 years.
Jefferson called it his "essay in architecture," and when a
visitor once commented on the incomplete work, he
responded, "And so I hope it will remain during my
life, as architecture is my delight, and putting up, and
pulling down, one of my favorite amusements."

For the most part, Jefferson rejected the architectural
traditions established in Virginia. His object at Monticello
was to return to a stricter application of classical sources
and the Roman architectural orders as he understood
them from the 16th-century architect and theorist Andrea
Palladio. The facade of Monticello was essentially an
exercise in the use of the orders. Other examples of
Jefferson's interest in classicism were his designs for an
octagonal chapel and the remodeling of the Governor's
Palace (1706–20), Williamsburg, which called for the
addition of pedimented porticoes; neither design was
implemented.

While in Europe on a diplomatic mission from 1784
until 1789, Jefferson was profoundly influenced by French
neoclassism. A tour of ancient ruins in southern France
prompted his comment that "Roman taste, genius, and
magnificence excite ideas." When asked in 1785 to
submit a design for the Virginia State Capitol (1785–98),
Richmond, he chose as his source the Corinthian temple
at Nimes known as the Maison Carrée. Jefferson's design
is among the first to envision a government body housed
in a classical temple. As secretary of state and later as
president, he continued to promote the idea of neoclassical architecture for public buildings.

In 1796 he began to enlarge and remodel Monticello,
and although he preserved the Palladian context of the
architectural orders, he abandoned much of the rigid
academic approach to classicism. The final design reflects
in plan and elevation what Jefferson learned from the
rational planning of the newest houses in and about Paris.

Thomas Jefferson, pencil sketch, c. 1799, once owned by Benjamin H. Latrobe. (Maryland Historical Society)

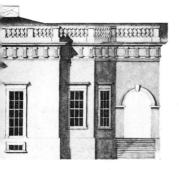

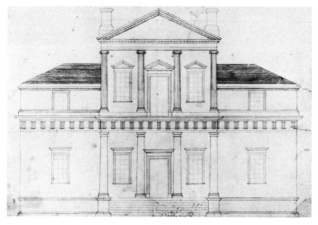

Middle and above: Jefferson's original design for Monticello, showing superimposed Ionic and Doric porticoes, and a contemporary view. The changes reflect the evolution of Jefferson's ideas about architecture. (Massachusetts Historical Society; Edwin S. Roseberry)

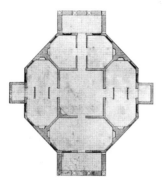

Virginia State Capitol (1785–98), Richmond, an early adaptation of a Roman temple to a modern purpose. (Virginia State Library)

Elevation (1792–93) of the President's House (The White House). Jefferson's design was inspired by Palladio's Villa Rotunda. (Massachusetts Historical Society)

Plan of Poplar Forest (1806–19), Lynchburg, Va., Jefferson's octagonal house. (Massachusetts Historical Society)

Opposite and below: Pavilion IX and the University of Virginia (1817–26), Charlottesville, Jefferson's "academical village." The pavilions were to be "models of taste and good architecture, and of a variety of appearance, no two alike." (University of Virginia; Michael J. Cronin)

Other designs dating after his return from Europe include several courthouses, a chuch (no longer standing), houses for friends, an octagonal house for his own use, Poplar Forest (1806–19), near Lynchburg, Va., and the University of Virginia (1817–26), Charlottesville. The university was his greatest achievement as an architect: Not only was he the founder of the institution, but he was also the architect of all the original buildings. He conceived it as "an academical village," and in the development of the design he solicited ideas from Benjamin H. Latrobe and William Thornton. Latrobe suggested a rotunda as the dominant feature, and Jefferson adopted the idea, designing a half-scale adaptation of the Pantheon in Rome. The Rotunda, used as a library, was flanked by wings forming a U-shaped composition of 10 pavilions for classrooms and professors' quarters, linked by a colonnade behind which were the dormitories.

Monticello was far too personal and idiosyncratic to have any noticeable influence on American architecture, but the direction toward classicism that Jefferson encouraged in public architecture had a lasting effect. At the time he sent his design for the Virginia State Capitol from Paris he wrote, "You see I am an enthusiast on the subject of the arts. But it is an enthusiasm of which I am not ashamed, as its object is to improve the taste of my countrymen, to increase their reputation, to reconcile to them the respect of the world and procure them its praise." ◺

ROBERT MILLS
John M. Bryan

Robert Mills (1781–1855) claimed to be the first native-born American to train specifically for an architectural career. He took drafting lessons as a youth in Charleston, S.C., and at the age of 19 went to Washington, D.C., to work for James Hoban, who was then directing construction of the White House and U.S. Capitol. In 1802 Mills won $150 in the design competition for the South Carolina College, his first public recognition.

While in Washington, Mills was befriended by Thomas Jefferson, who introduced him to Benjamin H. Latrobe, and from 1803 until 1809 Mills worked for Latrobe—first as an apprentice, or draftsman, and then as a clerk of the works, or job superintendent—on many projects, including the Chesapeake and Delaware Canal, the Baltimore cathedral and the Bank of Philadelphia. Increasing confidence and professional contacts soon led to his own commissions, and by 1810 Mills and Latrobe were drifting apart.

Mills had moved to Philadelphia in 1808, where he designed three auditoriums—the Washington Hall (1809–16), the Sansom Street Baptist Church (1811–12) and the Octagon Unitarian Church (1812–17). In 1812 he gained national recognition for a similar undertaking in Richmond, Va., for a design that won over one by Latrobe. The Monumental Church combined features that would become hallmarks of his style—an octagonal plan (reflecting a concern for sight lines and acoustics), a daring saucer dome, interior ornament and a principal Doric porch, the latter two especially original, bold and massive in character.

Mills also won a national competition for the Baltimore Washington Monument (1814–42), a colossal

Robert Mills, from a daguerreotype made about 1851. (Jessie H. Whitehurst, National Portrait Gallery, Smithsonian Institution)

Unexecuted plan (1802) for the South Carolina College, Columbia, featuring a distinctive arcaded walkway at ground level. (South Carolina Department of Archives and History)

Top and above: Mills's original
design for the Baltimore Washington Monument (1814–42) and the
monument as built. (Maryland Historical Society; A. Aubrey Bodine
Collection, Peale Museum)

Elevation of the Fireproof Building (1821), Charleston, S.C. Mills's design reflects his interest in fireproof, masonry vaulted construction. (South Carolina Historical Society)

160-foot column that was the first major memorial to the president. To direct this work he moved to Baltimore in 1815, but a depression disrupted the building trades in 1819, and, finding himself destitute, he accepted an offer to direct public improvements for the state of South Carolina.

Throughout the early 1820s he labored in South Carolina, building canals, courthouses, jails, hospitals and offices, always emphasizing utility and sound construction. The state legislature abolished his office in 1823, and, struggling to support his family, he produced a detailed, county-by-county map of the state and an accompanying descriptive volume, both landmarks in the analysis of American topography.

Seeking federal employment, he moved to Washington in 1830. Success seemed assured when, in 1836, his design for the Washington Monument (1848–84) was accepted. His fourth public monument based on an Egyptian obelisk, it is indubitably among the most impressive achievements of American architecture. Also in 1836, Andrew Jackson approved Mills's design for a new, fireproof Treasury Building; its Ionic colonnade is his

Treasury Building (1836–69), Washington, D.C., an influential Greek Revival design featuring a dramatic Ionic colonnade and using fireproof construction. (General Services Administration)

Opposite: Robert Mills House (1823–25), Columbia, S.C., a Palladian design that is also known as Ainsley Hall. (Richard A. Shackelford)

Right and below: Washington Monument (1848–84), Washington, D.C., the most prominent evidence of the Egyptian Revival style in America, although Mills's design was significantly altered in execution. The capstone was finished in place. (HABS; Jack E. Boucher, HABS)

most grand Greek Revival elevation. Neither the Monument nor the Treasury Building was finished as he intended; their alterations are symptomatic of the political and economic problems that plagued the final phase of his career.

Mills was involved in virtually every major project in Washington throughout the 1830s and 1840s. As the architect of public buildings, he worked on the Patent Office (1836–40) in an uneasy relationship with its designers—William Parker Elliot, Ithiel Town and Alexander J. Davis. He began the Old Post Office (1839–42) and supervised construction of the Smithsonian Institution (1847–55), which had been designed by James Renwick. Congress abolished his office in 1842, but he continued to work on specific commissions. Finally, in 1851, a controversy concerning work at the Patent Office and Capitol precipitated his departure, at age 70, from federal service. A younger generation of architects, including Ammi B. Young and Thomas U. Walter, took his place, but his legacy has remained a formative influence in American architecture.

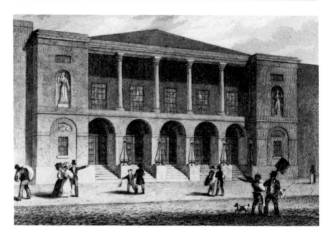

WILLIAM STRICKLAND
Nancy Halverson Schless

William Strickland (1788–1854) was a designer of "utmost good taste" and one who "never sacrificed solidity for show—the useful for the merely ornamental," boasted the commissioners for the Tennessee State Capitol in 1845 about their architect. Indeed, the quality of Strickland's prodigious output—more than 50 commissions executed in almost a half century of practice in Philadelphia, along the eastern seaboard and in Tennessee—merits the commissioners' praise. Ebullient and volatile in character, virtuosic and creative in temperament, he was active as an engineer, surveyor, painter and scene painter, engraver and aquatinter, author and city planner as well as architect. Strickland designed exquisitely graceful build-ings in nine styles, but his major contribution to 19th-century architecture was his inauguration of the Greek Revival based on the pure temple form, a movement that was to dominate American building from 1820 to 1850.

Born the son of a carpenter in Navesink, N.J., and brought to Philadelphia by 1790, Strickland served a stormy apprenticeship to Benjamin H. Latrobe from 1803 to 1805. After working as a scene designer in New York, he returned to Philadelphia "as a sort of artist in general." During his earliest period, he designed only five buildings, the most notable his maiden offering, the Gothic Revival Masonic Hall (1808–11), Philadelphia, with a 180-foot wooden steeple.

In 1818 Strickland was catapulted to fame when his strictly Grecian design won the competition for the Second Bank of the United States, Philadelphia, the first public building based on the Parthenon as illustrated in James Stuart and Nicholas Revett's *Antiquities of Athens, Measured and Delineated* (1762). He evoked other styles with such works as the Gothic Revival St. Stephen's Episcopal Church (1822–23) and his Federal-style Second Chestnut Street Theater (1820–22), both in Philadelphia. Recognition of his prowess as an engineer came in 1825, when the Pennsylvania Society for the Promotion of Internal Improvements sent him on a nine-month study tour of British transportation systems.

Strickland's mature career reads like a typical Ameri-can success story. The architect emerged as an author with the 1826 publication of his *Reports*. Again courted as

Opposite: Second Chestnut Street
Theater (1820–22), Philadelphia, a
Federal-style theater featuring an
arcaded ground story supporting a
colonnade. (Fenner, Sears and Company, Free Library of Philadelphia)

William Strickland, by John Neagle,
1829. (Mabel Brady Garvan Collection, Yale University Art Gallery)

Second Bank of the United States
(1818–24), Philadelphia, the first
adaptation of the Parthenon's Doric
form to the functions of a 19th-
century American public building.
(Jack E. Boucher, HABS)

U.S. Mint (1829–33), Philadelphia, a Greek Revival building whose widely
spaced Ionic portico contrasts with the horizontal emphasis. (W. H. Hay,
Free Library of Philadelphia)

Masonic Hall (1808–11), Philadelphia, an important building in the early Gothic Revival style, decorated with picturesque buttresses, pinnacles and thin moldings. (Historical Society of Pennsylvania)

U.S. Naval Asylum (U.S. Naval Home) (1827–33), Philadelphia. The broad central Ionic portico balances piazzas along the wings, which allow for ventilation. (Wild and Chevalier, Athenaeum of Philadelphia)

an engineer, he supervised the Delaware Breakwater (1828–40), which still protects Philadelphia's harbor, and he undertook a pioneer restoration project for Independence Hall in 1828 by designing a replica of the first steeple, which had been removed. And with his notable series of Philadelphia Greek Revival buildings of the 1820s and 1830s, he continued to make a national classicism ever more acceptable to Americans of that era who had an idealized view of the democratic city-state of antiquity. Strickland was always an archeologist at second hand through the medium of published works—he never visited Greece—but he was no pedant. The Philadelphia (Merchants') Exchange (1832–34) reflects his sensitivity to the subtleties and decorative richness of Greek Corinthian form.

After the panic of 1837 and the depression in the East, Strickland was delighted to accept commissions in Tennessee. His final works reflect bold monumentality as in the Egyptian Revival Downtown (First) Presbyterian Church (1848–51), Nashville. The apex of his career, the Tennessee State Capitol (1845–59), Nashville, is an imposing design of great height and scale, composed of diverse classical elements. As a controlled synthesis of various antique forms, the capitol (where Strickland is buried) heralds the age of picturesque eclecticism.

During his career as a first-generation professional architect, Strickland was a worthy heir to Latrobe. Through his pupils, Gideon Shryock and Thomas U. Walter, he was to continue to play a key role in reshaping American architectural taste.

Philadelphia (Merchants')
Exchange (1832–34), distinguished
by a dramatically curved colonnade
capped by a classical lantern. (Philadelphia Museum of Art)

Downtown (First) Presbyterian
Church (1848–51), Nashville, one of
Strickland's three Egyptian Revival
designs, featuring a winged-disk
motif, reeded columns and palm
capitals. (Jack E. Boucher, HABS)

Tennessee State Capitol (1845–59), Nashville, dramatically sited on an
urban hillside and composed of forceful, interlocking forms defined by four
Ionic porticoes. (Tennessee Historical Commission)

JOHN HAVILAND
Jeffrey A. Cohen

English-born John Haviland (1792–1852) arrived in Philadelphia in the fall of 1816, just after Robert Mills and
William Strickland had achieved their earliest professional
successes in that city. With them and a few others,
Haviland would become one of the principal figures in a
heroic age of American architecture, when a hunger for
communal celebration in monumental form gripped the
popular consciousness and architects enjoyed an un-
paralleled degree of personal recognition for designing
such concrete symbols. His works combined a firm
neoclassical taste with a vigor and range generally
unmatched during America's Greek Revival.

Haviland had trained in London under the architect
James Elmes and had briefly sought his fortune in Russia
before coming to this country. Almost immediately he
began to teach architecture and draftsmanship, and
between 1818 and 1821 produced *The Builder's Assistant*,
the first American publication to detail the ancient Greek
versions of the classical orders. This work appeared at a
fluid moment in American taste, however, before the
formal constancy of the Greek Revival began to over-
shadow all else. The few professional architects in this
country were departing distinctly and self-consciously
from traditional local norms and were turning instead to
the sudden wealth of architectural examples published
abroad that detailed historically and geographically diverse
styles. These met with approval from a public eager to see
itself as more cosmopolitan, and Haviland exploited this
taste for stylistic novelty with works that borrowed boldly
from medieval, oriental, Egyptian, Roman and Greek
styles. He controlled such diversity by a tendency toward
geometrically idealized volumes arranged in symmetrical
but additive compositions, while Roman planning and
arched, vaulted and domed systems reigned internally.

For Haviland and other architects, however, the Greek
classicism rediscovered in the pages of Stuart and Revett's
landmark publication, *Antiquities of Athens,* asserted a
primacy over these varied styles. At first only isolated
details of this classicism were adopted, but in the early
1820s Haviland briefly indulged in a more comprehensive
kind of Greek revivalism that appears to have anticipated
the widespread adoption of that style in America as a
national imagery. But he just as quickly reverted to his
eclectic approach, using Roman forms externally long
after his American-born colleagues had discarded them for
a more exclusively Greek appearance. This change may
have been due partly to a more circumspect European
attitude toward the style, but it probably also reflected his
love of novelty evident in his early advocacy of the
commercial arcade, as in the Philadelphia Arcade
(1825–28); the cast-iron facade, as in the Miner's Bank
(1830–31), Pottsville, Pa.; the colonnaded residential row,
as in Colonnade Row (1830), Philadelphia; the radial
penitentiary, as in the Eastern State Penitentiary
(1821–37), Philadelphia; and the Egyptian style, as in the
Halls of Justice and House of Detention (The Tombs)
(1835–38), New York.

Despite his accomplishments, Haviland's career did not
proceed smoothly. Like Benjamin H. Latrobe two decades

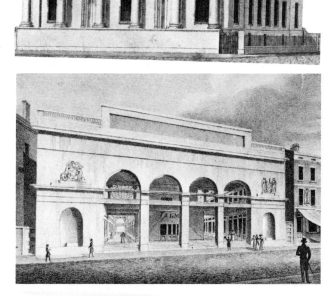

First Presbyterian Church (1820–22), Philadelphia, one of the earliest American churches cast as a Greek temple. (Atwater Kent Museum)

Philadelphia Arcade (1825–28), Philadelphia. A speculative scheme initiated by Haviland and a partner, the arcade housed two levels of shops fronting on two glass-roofed corridors. (William Birch, Free Library of Philadelphia)

John Haviland, with a plan and perspective of the Eastern State Penitentiary, by John Neagle, 1828. (Metropolitan Museum of Art)

earlier, Haviland entertained expectations of a gentlemanly lifestyle that were confounded by a dearth of paying clients. Driven to speculative business ventures, he twice went bankrupt. His prison designs—particularly for Eastern State Penitentiary and The Tombs—along with his repeated use of the Egyptian style brought widespread patronage and emulation. Toward midcentury, however, the tides of architectural taste were changing in fundamental ways, leaving behind Haviland the neoclassicist, the innovative planner and the mercurial eclectic. ◿

Eastern State Penitentiary
(1821–37), Philadelphia, the internationally acclaimed prototype of the
radial-plan prison, with a castel-
lated Gothic facade and cell blocks
for solitary confinement radiating
from a central rotunda. (HABS)

Franklin Institute (Atwater Kent
Museum) (1825–26), Philadelphia.
The classical facade may have reflected the building's mission—the
study of science and the mechanical arts, including architecture.
(Atwater Kent Museum)

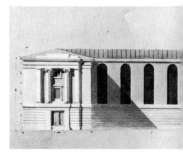

Proposed design (1833) of the Pennsylvania Hospital, Philadelphia. The
dome and arcade show Haviland's
variations within the Greek Revival
style. (Pennsylvania Hospital)

Chinese Pagoda and Labyrinth Garden (1828), Philadelphia. This suburban
recreation structure, with its oriental detail and picturesque arrangement,
still retains a classical sense of order. (Lucas, Atwater Kent Museum)

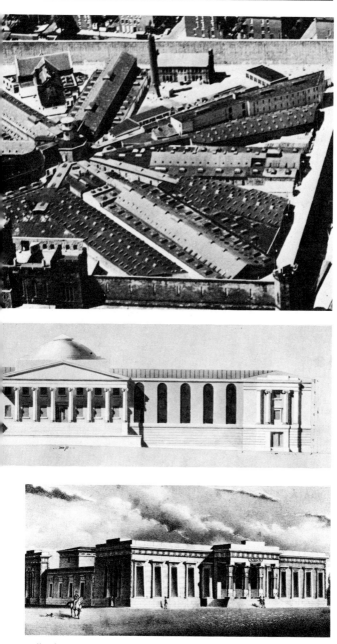

Halls of Justice and House of Detention (The Tombs) (1835–38), New York, a prison modeled on Egyptian monuments "rediscovered" during Napoleon's conquest of Egypt. (New York Public Library)

RICHARD UPJOHN
Phoebe Stanton

Richard Upjohn (1802–78) was particularly influential in establishing the revivals of medieval and Italianate styles in the 19th century. He was a devout churchman, the architect of choice in a period of much church building. His exemplary professional deportment, his convictions about the role the practice of design should assume in the life of the nation and his belief that architecture deserved a place among the professions were instrumental in the founding of the American Institute of Architects in 1857 and the formulation of its intellectual objectives. Upjohn's work is distinguished by its sturdy integrity, its ingenuity and the way in which he adapted personal preferences in form to the style he was using.

Born in England, Upjohn came to the United States in 1829 and settled in New England, where he acquired architectural experience in the office of Alexander Parris, a Boston architect. His earliest buildings, modest commissions for houses and a church in Maine, illustrate his preoccupation with fundamentals of design and practicality rather than ornament. They also reveal his knowledge of English writers on architecture and its principles, a rich vein of materials on which he would continue to draw.

Upjohn's first major work, and the one for which he is best known, was Trinity Church in New York. From 1839, when he began to consult on its repair or rebuilding, until it was completed in 1846, Upjohn was preoccupied with Trinity. It established him as a leader among American architects and the Gothic Revival as the style best suited to the needs of the Protestant Episcopal Church, a significant client both in the work it proffered and the tastes it encouraged. A sequence of large and small churches by Upjohn followed, among them the Church of the Holy Communion (1844–46), New York, and St. Mary's Church (1846), Burlington, N.J. Prompted by more requests than he could satisfy for designing small churches, rectories and schoolhouses, Upjohn in 1852 published *Rural Architecture*, whose patterns were used throughout the United States. He also prepared designs for modest churches remarkable for their sensitive design and the elegant way in which he adjusted the Gothic style to local building materials, craftsmanship and his own preferences (he enjoyed simplicity and avoided applied decoration).

Richard Upjohn. (Library of Congress)

Trinity Church (1839–46), New York, one of the most famous monuments
of the Gothic Revival, showing a more complete understanding of medieval
forms than any other American building at that time. (Library of
Congress)

St. Mary's Church (1846), Burlington, N.J., resembling an English
parish church with its simple masonry, absence of superfluous detail
and broach spire. (Library of
Congress)

St. Thomas's Church (1849–51),
Amenia Union, N.Y., a brick
church from Upjohn's experimental
period. (Phoebe Stanton)

St. Paul's Church (1854–46), Baltimore, in the Italianate style. The
lofty campanile was never executed. (Maryland Historical Society)

Because he recognized that the Gothic style, although
suitable for country settings, was difficult in an urban
context, Upjohn began, even while working on Trinity
Church, to develop a vocabulary of Romanesque forms, of
which the Bowdoin College Chapel and Library (1845–55),
Brunswick, Maine, is his masterpiece. After an 1850
European study tour, in which he visited Germany,
France, Italy and England, he was convinced that the
Italianate, then popular in England, was an alternative to
the medieval styles. St. Paul's Church (1854–56), Baltimore, is a masterwork in this style.

Upjohn was also a remarkable designer of houses.
Mansions in Newport, such as Kingscote (1839), and in
the suburbs of New York and the small but effective
houses he proposed in his book illustrate his talent for
adapting style to purpose and the requirements of a new
society. ◪

Kingscote (1839), Newport, R.I., in the Italianate style that was to become almost standard in Upjohn's domestic work. The addition on the left was designed by Stanford White. (Robert Lautman)

Bowdoin College Chapel and Library (1845–55), Brunswick, Maine, designed with seats lining the sides of the chapel, facing one another. The library was originally located at the rear. (Bowdoin College)

Church of the Holy Communion (1844–46), New York, a simple design set off by a slender tower with a battlemented top. (Phoebe Stanton Collection)

St. John Chrysostom's Church (1851–53), Delafield, Wis., a wood parish church of the simple, inexpensive type that Upjohn developed for rural parishes. (Phoebe Stanton)

THOMAS U. WALTER
Robert B. Ennis

Born into a family of Philadelphia bricklayers, Thomas Ustick Walter (1804–87) was apprenticed to his father, J. S. Walter, during construction of William Strickland's Second Bank of the United States (1818–24) and later became his father's business partner. With aspirations toward professional practice in architecture, in 1824 he entered the newly founded architecture school opened by the Franklin Institute under the direction of John Haviland. Four years later Walter became a draftsman in Strickland's office, where he remained until 1831, when he began his own practice.

During the next 12 years Walter produced more than 200 projects (half the total product of his career), mostly in Philadelphia and its environs, but also as far away as Maine and South Carolina. Most were in the Greek Revival style, such as the Chester County Bank (1835), West Chester, Pa., and the Matthew Newkirk House (1835), Philadelphia. Some were Gothic Revival, such as the Philadelphia County (Moyamensing) Prison (1831–35), and others were Egyptian Revival, such as the Debtor's Apartment (1835–36) at Moyamensing, although their forms always remained classical.

His most notable building of this early period was the Girard College for Orphans (1833–48), Philadelphia. In preparing its design, he was associated with Nicholas Biddle, the president of the Second Bank and one of the foremost shapers of American public taste, particularly in his espousal of Greek forms as best suited for the architectural expression of the American spirit. For him Walter executed the templelike extension (1833–41) of Andalusia, his country house near Philadelphia, and their friendship brought Walter a reputation for taste as well as for skill in building, business acumen and command of architectural theory.

The scarcity of commissions following the closing of the U. S. Bank in 1841 ended the first phase of Walter's career. His fortunes were revived by the commission in 1843–45 to construct the breakwater at La Guaira, Venezuela, and he enjoyed a second period of practice at home, during which he produced a few designs in the newly popular picturesque and Renaissance modes—Ingleside (1851), a house in Washington, D.C., and the new facade of the Spruce Street Baptist Church (1851), Philadelphia.

Girard College for Orphans (1833–48), Philadelphia, which epitomized the American Greek Revival. (The Athenaeum of Philadelphia)

Matthew Newkirk House (1835), Philadelphia. (The Athenaeum of Philadelphia)

Thomas U. Walter, c. 1870. (The Athenaeum of Philadelphia)

Chester County Bank (1835), West Chester, Pa. (The Athenaeum of Philadelphia)

In 1851 Walter won the competition for the extension of the U.S. Capitol. The addition of the new north and south wings so lengthened the building that the need for a new dome was quickly perceived. Designed by Walter by 1855, it was built of cast iron during the Civil War years, becoming a symbol of the unity of the American states, stimulating the American building industry and establishing Walter's standing as the most important and respected American architect of his day. While in Washington, D.C., he designed additional government buildings and contributed to expansions of still others (such as the Treasury Building and the old Patent and Post offices), as well as designing a number of houses for public figures.

His retirement to Philadelphia after 1865 was cut short by the panic of 1873, and Walter was briefly reduced to working as a draftsman in the architectural office of the Pennsylvania Railroad. He was involved in planning the Centennial Exhibition of 1876, and until his death he was in charge of the construction of John McArthur's design for the Philadelphia City Hall (1871–1901), probably contributing the cast-iron uppermost portion of the tower. Walter's death in 1887 left the American architectural profession in mourning. It owed him much: The creation of the American Institute of Architects, which finally established the profession in the United States, had been his inspiration in 1835, and he had been one of the 11 persons who brought it into being in 1857. ◣

Ingleside (1851), Washington, D.C., an Italianate villa inspired by Andrew Jackson Downing. (The Athenaeum of Philadelphia)

Philadelphia County (Moyamensing) Prison (1831–35), Philadelphia, in the Gothic Revival style, and the Debtor's Apartment (1835–36), in the Egyptian Revival style. (The Athenaeum of Philadelphia; Jack E. Boucher, HABS)

Andalusia (additions 1833–41), near Philadelphia, one of the most noted Greek Revival houses in America. (Jack E. Boucher, HABS)

Extension and cast-iron dome (1851–65), U.S. Capitol, under construction during the Civil War years. The completion of Walter's dome symbolized the continuation of the nation. (Architect of the Capitol Collection, Library of Congress; The Athenaeum of Philadelphia)

JAMES RENWICK
Selma Rattner

James Renwick (1818–95) began at the top. He was only 24 years old when he won the commission for New York's Grace Church (1843–46), an event equal to being named architect of a major corporate skyscraper today. During the next 50 years, Renwick designed outstanding churches, including the internationally acclaimed St. Patrick's Cathedral (1858–79, spires 1885–88), museums, schools, theaters, hotels, commercial buildings and city and country houses throughout the United States.

Renwick had talent, ambition and, like many of his colleagues, social and educational advantages. Born into America's influential upper class and a graduate of Columbia College, he was trained as an engineer by his father, who helped him obtain his first jobs as an engineer while encouraging him to pursue a career in architecture. In 1851 Renwick married Anna Lloyd Aspinwall, daughter of one of the richest men in America. Substantial private and professional income provided for an elegant lifestyle. Nonetheless, Renwick devoted himself to his practice and to the training of apprentices, such as Bertram Goodhue.

From the outset, Renwick had the knowledge and self-confidence to be inventive. Grace Church and Trinity Church (1839–46, Richard Upjohn), both completed in the same year, were the first credible American adaptations of the medieval Gothic mode, but Renwick's lavish white marble design was more original, combining French as well as the customary English motifs and designed in an unprecedented cruciform shape. Structurally, too, Renwick was a leader. St. Patrick's Cathedral was planned with a stone tower over the crossing supported by the first giant masonry vault ever built in the United States; a plaster vault was substituted because of mounting costs but only after the necessary (and now meaningless) flying buttresses had been completed.

Renwick quickly gained celebrity status for his stylistic and technical competence. His Romanesque entry was selected for the Smithsonian's "Castle" (1847–55), Washington, D.C., the first American public building in that style. Two months later he adopted a Gothic design for the Free Academy (1847–49), later the College of the City of New York. By the 1850s Renwick's reputation extended to hotel design: The Clarendon

Opposite: The "Castle" (1847–55), Smithsonian Institution, Washington, D.C., the first American public building in the Romanesque style. Renwick originally proposed a more substantial structural system, not implemented because of lack of funds. (Jeff Tinsley, Smithsonian Institution)

Grace Church (1843–46) and Rectory (1847), New York, both in the Gothic Revival style. As church architect, Renwick ensured the stylistic continuity of all additions and alterations. (Private collection)

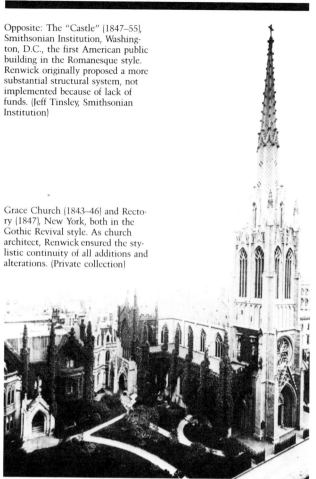

James Renwick. (Avery Architectural and Fine Arts Library, Columbia University)

St. Denis Hotel (c. 1851–52), New York, a fashionable "Elizabethan" hotel that reflects Renwick's personal taste. (Museum of the City of New York)

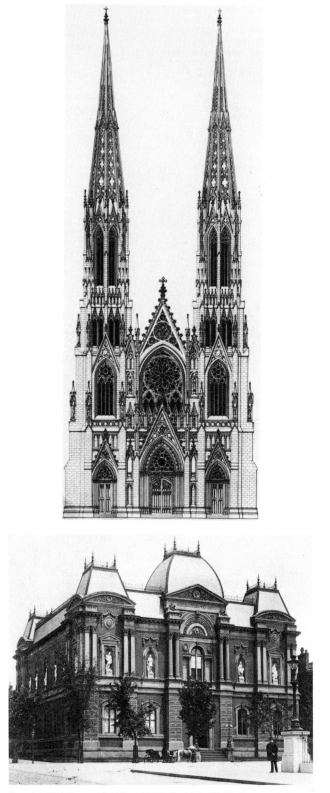

Renwick (Old Corcoran) Gallery (1859–61, 1870–71), Washington, D.C. Renwick's use of red brick produced a uniquely American variation of the Second Empire style. (James C. Massey Collection)

Opposite: Elevation of St. Patrick's Cathedral (1858–79, 1885–88), New York, a structurally innovative design. (Avery Architectural and Fine Arts Library, Columbia University)

Booth's Theater (1867–69), New York, a Second Empire–style building with advanced mechanical equipment. (Museum of the City of New York)

Island Hospital (1858–61), New York, designed in the Second Empire style but without excessive ornamentation. (New-York Historical Society)

(1850–51) and the St. Denis (c. 1851–52), derived from Italianate and Elizabethan forms, and the palatial Albemarle (1859–62), all in New York, were begun in that decade. His diversified talent enabled him to create castles for aspiring "English lords," chateaux for Francophiles and Federal-style mansions for clients proud of their early American lineage.

Among the many important accomplishments in Renwick's prolific career was the introduction of the Second Empire style for public buildings. He first used it for the Island Hospital (1858–61), New York, and perfected it in the original Corcoran (now Renwick) Gallery (1859–61, 1870–71), Washington, D.C., Vassar College (1861–65), Poughkeepsie, N.Y., and Booth's Theater (1867–69), New York, famous also for its sophisticated mechanical equipment.

Renwick's use of technology was, in fact, as conspicuous as his stylistic virtuosity. In addition to improved mechanical systems, he was among the first to employ new building materials such as wrought iron for complete floor framing and durable terra cotta for exterior ornament.

In 1890, at the age of 72, Renwick undertook a design for the proposed National Gallery of History and Art in Washington, D.C., a huge outdoor museum complex. Although never built, the monumental Beaux-Arts classical layout was revolutionary both as the stylistic forerunner of the celebrated 1893 World's Columbian Exposition and for the early use of reinforced concrete as the chief building material. This kind of vision and the courage to experiment characterized Renwick's entire career.

ORSON SQUIRE FOWLER
W. Ray Luce

Orson Squire Fowler (1809–87) was not an architect or a builder but the nation's leading phrenologist. His most lasting contribution was his book, *A Home for All*, which established the octagon as a new, particularly American house plan, popularized an early form of concrete and sought to combine social and architectural goals to provide substantial, economical housing for all Americans.

Born in Cohocton, N.Y., Fowler studied for the ministry at Amherst College. Following graduation, he began lecturing and writing on phrenology, the study of the conformation of the skull to determine a person's character, and quickly became the country's foremost advocate. He lectured and wrote extensively also on topics from diet and health to love and marriage.

Fowler entered architecture with the same confidence with which he gave advice on almost any topic. He wrote *A Home for All* (1848) after planning his own house and writing a series of articles on phrenological character traits, including constructiveness. Fowler based his architectural model on the circle, which he felt was nature's building form and which enclosed the greatest interior space with the least exterior wall. A circular structure, however, was difficult to build, whereas most builders could construct an octagon. Fowler claimed that the octagonal plan was wholly original, although he probably had seen octagonal schools and churches along the Hudson River and in southeastern Pennsylvania. He probably did not know about Jefferson's octagonal house, Poplar Forest (1806–19), near Lynchburg, Va.

A Home for All also included advice on other building concerns. In the first edition, Fowler advocated walls made of rough-cut stacked lumber, but in the second edition, published in 1853, he favored an early form of concrete he discovered in Milton, Wis. The second edition, which went through numerous printings, promoted the gravel wall octagon as well as recent inventions

Orson Squire Fowler House (1850–53), Fishkill, N.Y., an imposing four-story residence whose balconies provide the architectural focus. (*A Home for All*)

such as the gravity water system, central heating and ventilating systems, speaking tubes, dumbwaiters and indoor bathrooms. The book also covered energy conservation, room placement to save steps and landscaping.

Fowler's goals were social as well as architectural. His purpose was proclaimed by his book's title as well as in its preface: "To cheapen and improve human homes, and especially to bring comfortable dwellings within the reach of the poorer classes, is the object of this volume."

Although Fowler included the plans for several octagons in his book, he built only one, his own house (1850–53) in Fishkill, N.Y., a three-story octagon with more than 60 rooms overlooking the Hudson River. Fowler's book created the octagon fad and led to the construction of octagons from coast to coast. The greatest concentration of octagons built before the Civil War is found in New York and New England, but octagons were recorded in almost 40 states and continued to be built until almost 1900.

Octagonal houses represent an important American architectural legacy. They may well be the first truly American architecture, for they were not derived from European precedents (Europe had octagonal buildings but not octagonal houses). Moreover, Fowler's amateur experimentation, his concern for the common people and his search for natural building patterns are central themes in American architecture. ◣

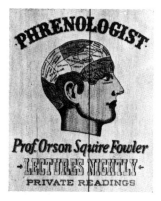

Advertisement for a lecture by Orson Squire Fowler.

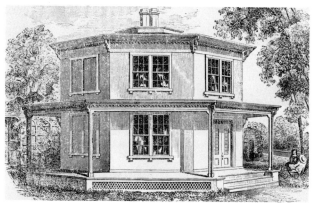

John J. Brown House (c. 1853), Williamsburgh, N.Y., a small two-story octagonal cottage with classical and Italianate detailing. *(A Home for All)*

Floor plan for a 27-foot octagonal house, showing variety of room shapes, convenience of arrangements and economy of effort Fowler claimed for the octagonal plan. (*A Home for All*)

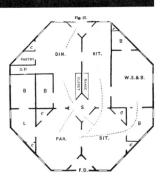

Milton House (1844), Milton, Wis., a hexagonal house of grout, an early form of concrete, which Fowler advocated in the second edition of his book. (HABS)

Longwood (1860–62), near Natchez, Miss., an ornate octagon with two-story verandas and a large onion dome on a 16-sided lantern. (Mabel Lane)

Armour-Stiner House (1859–60), Irvington, N.Y., a grand octagon reflecting an eclectic combination of elements from the Gothic, Stick, Second Empire and Eastlake styles. (Thom Loughman, HABS)

McElroy House (1861, Warren Charles Perry), San Francisco, made of concrete with clapboard siding with Italianate details.

Octagonal school (1886), District No. 9, Marcellus, N.Y., showing the room arrangement from the interior. (HABS)

ALEXANDER J. DAVIS
Jane B. Davies

At the time when American romanticism was flourishing in literature and Hudson River landscape painting, Alexander J. Davis (1803–92) brought a similar spirit of romanticism to American architecture. Imaginative, original and influential, he was an innovative leader in the important styles of the middle third of the 19th century—the Greek, Tuscan and Gothic revivals, the Italianate and the bracketed. Although he never studied or even traveled abroad, he created inventive American interpretations inspired by foreign sources, designing with adept versatility some of the finest buildings of the period.

The adventurous imagination, temperament, eye and skill of an artist gave Davis's work a special quality. He began as an architectural illustrator, and his approach to architecture was always visual. He was primarily a designer, constantly experimenting, excellent in composition, proportion and detail, with a scenic sense for the harmony of building and setting and for the drama of bold features and strong contrasts. His skillful watercolors are considered among the finest architectural renderings of his generation.

Although Davis lived in New York City most of his life, his work ranged from Maine to Florida, from Detroit to New Orleans. He designed buildings in many styles and of many types—public, institutional and commercial buildings, churches and chapels, and town, suburban and country houses.

During two periods—1829–35 and 1842–43—Davis was a partner of the eminent Ithiel Town, who had the greatest architectural library in America. Most of their buildings were advanced examples of the new Greek Revival style, as seen, for instance, in the bold temple-form Indiana State Capitol (1831–35), Indianapolis, and in the typically Davis multistory windows of the Lyceum of Natural History (1835–36), New York. Throughout his career Davis continued to use his characteristic windows with neoclassical styles for most institutional and urban buildings, often favoring the wide eaves and strong features of individualistic versions of the Tuscan style, as in the Bridgeport City Hall (1853–54), Bridgeport, Conn.

Federal Hall National Memorial (U.S. Custom House) (1833–42, with Ithiel Town), New York, an American adaptation of the Parthenon. (HABS)

Alexander J. Davis, by George Freeman, 1852. (Avery Architectural and Fine Arts Library, Columbia University)

By midcentury Davis was the outstanding American architect of romantic country houses, unsurpassed in his mastery of asymmetrical massing, control of scale and delicacy of detailing. He designed many of the earliest and finest American villas and cottages in the Gothic Revival, Italianate and bracketed styles, such as Henry Delamater's charming Gothic cottage (1844), Rhinebeck, N.Y.; the enchanting Gothic villa Belmead (1845–48) for Philip St. George Cocke in Powhatan County, Va.; Llewellyn S. Haskell's handsome Italianate villa, Belmont (1850–52), near Belleville, N.J.; and the Gothic splendor of Lyndhurst (1838–42, 1865–67), Tarrytown, N.Y.

Davis's influence spread widely through his works and his book, *Rural Residences* (1838), and through his collaboration from 1839 to 1850 with the tastemaker Andrew Jackson Downing on the latter's publications, for which Davis drew most of the architectural illustrations—his own designs, a few supplied by other architects and many created jointly by Davis and Downing. The English ideas of the picturesque, which they espoused, revolutionized the American house, relating it to its setting, giving irregularity to its shape, plan and surface and freeing it from the austere rigidity of the traditional box pattern. The diversity of the new styles enriched the American scene. Many of the forms and features were imitated so much that they passed into the vernacular, and some—such as asymmetrical massing, bay windows, board-and-batten siding, wide decorated eaves and expansive verandas—became lasting contributions to American domestic architecture. ◹

North Carolina State Capitol (1833–40, with Ithiel Town et al.), Raleigh, with giant Doric columns and antae. (North Carolina Museum of History)

Below and middle: William J. Rotch House (1845–46), New Bedford,
Mass., a cottage villa in the rural Gothic style, rendered by Davis. The
dramatic design and intricate, elegant ornamentation give it exceptional
charm. (Avery Architectural and Fine Arts Library, Columbia University;
Metropolitan Museum of Art)

Lyndhurst (1838–42, 1865–67), Tarrytown, N.Y., the culmination of Hudson
River Gothic, rendered by Davis. (Metropolitan Museum of Art)

Gatehouse at Blithewood (1836), near Barrytown, N.Y., the prototypal American Gothic cottage. (Avery Architectural and Fine Arts Library, Columbia University)

Davis's design for a cottage villa in the bracketed style, featuring bracketed eaves and veranda supports and his distinctive windows, from Andrew Jackson Downing's *Cottage Residences* (1842).

Davis's preliminary design for Grace Hill (1854–57), Brooklyn, N.Y., featuring a radiating, interconnected plan. (New-York Historical Society)

ANDREW JACKSON DOWNING
George B. Tatum

When she praised a number of the villas and cottages encountered on her American tour of 1849–50, the Swedish novelist Fredrika Bremer was advised that the architectural qualities she admired might be traced to the writings of Andrew Jackson Downing (1815–52), the popular landscape gardener from Newburgh, N.Y. "Nobody, whether he be rich or poor, builds a house or lays out a garden without consulting Downing's works," she was told.

Although Downing had contributed to the American editions of the works of several English authors and his own writings on the fruits of the United States had assured him a respected place among pomologists, it was clearly to his role as architecture critic that Bremer's informant referred. His *Treatise on the Theory and Practice of Landscape Gardening Adapted to North America* (1841) contained a long section on rural architecture, which was also the subject of a smaller volume entitled *Cottage Residences*, published the following year. The success of both books was immediate. Together with later essays in *The Horticulturist*, the journal Downing edited from its inception in 1846 until his untimely death in a steamboat explosion in 1852, and *The Architecture of Country Houses* (1850), Downing's third and last major work dealing with architectural subjects, these two publications did much to establish their author as a kind of arbiter of taste. Soon houses adapted from their illustrations appeared throughout the American countryside, and numerous imitators brought out a variety of pattern books based on this new approach to architectural design.

Much of Downing's practical knowledge of horticulture was gained in the Newburgh nursery he and his brother had inherited from their father, but the artistic principles he advocated were largely distilled from English sources, especially the publications of John Claudius Loudon. To illustrate his writings, Downing occasionally used the work of contemporary architects such as Richard Upjohn or John Notman, but he depended principally on Alexander J. Davis, who not only provided examples of his own work but also undertook to transform Downing's rough sketches into finished drawings suitable for engraving. Classical elements made the Italianate style appropriate for sites near towns or cities, but the irregular terrain of the countryside called for the more picturesque forms of the Gothic. And should either of these styles prove too ambitious, Downing recommended the simpler bracketed mode, derived ostensibly from Swiss and Italian sources and as near an original American style as the period was to come.

Downing advertised that for $50 he would furnish landscape drawings by mail, and for $20 a day he was prepared to visit the site. Plans supplied in this way were probably destroyed in use; at least, none is known to survive, and the loss or destruction of Downing's office records has deprived us of a list of his clients. Matthew Vassar was one, and contemporary views and descriptions provide a good deal of information about Springside (1850–52), the Vassar estate near Poughkeepsie, N.Y.,

Andrew Jackson Downing, from a daguerreotype made about 1850. (George B. Tatum Collection)

Unexecuted design (1847) by Alexander J. Davis in collaboration with Downing. Two years later Davis submitted a slightly modified version of this design to a client in Ohio, for whom it was built. (Metropolitan Museum of Art)

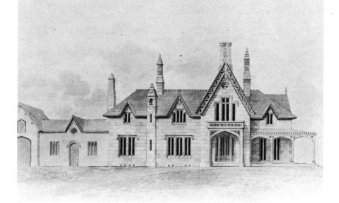

Daniel Parish House (1852), Newport, R.I., designed by Downing and Calvert Vaux in the new Renaissance style then coming into vogue in America.

only remnants of which are extant.

From time to time Downing served as consultant for a design drawn up in its final form by Davis, but he does not appear to have considered himself a practicing architect in his own right much before 1850. In the summer of that year, he had his first trip to England and, while there, persuaded young Calvert Vaux to immigrate to Newburgh as a member of the architectural firm he was in the process of forming. The new firm did not want for commissions, some of the most important of which were later published by Vaux in his *Villas and Cottages* (1857). Downing was the natural choice to provide a design for the public grounds in Washington, D.C., and although in 1901 the present Mall replaced the informal lines of his 1851 plan, both the early date and the success of the latter have led its designer to be counted among the originators of the public park in America.

Italianate villa, from Downing's *Cottage Residences*, usually considered the first example of this popular form published in America. Downing wrote that the campanile conferred a character of boldness and dignity.

Opposite: Plan for Springside (1850–52), near Poughkeepsie, N.Y. (Benson Lossing, *Life of Matthew Vassar*, 1876)

Downing's plan for the public grounds (1851), Washington, D.C., showing Robert Mills's original design for the Washington Monument. (Smith and Jenkins, Library of Congress)

Cottage in the English, or rural Gothic, style, one of the most copied designs in *Cottage Residences* and apparently based in large part on the work of Alexander J. Davis.

FREDERICK LAW OLMSTED
Laura Wood Roper

Frederick Law Olmsted (1822–1903), father of American landscape architecture, came late to his calling. Born in Hartford, Conn., and ill educated by a series of rural clergymen, he was successively a seaman, farmer, journalist and publisher, intermittently a traveler and always a lover and analyst of the rural scenery of his native region. His false starts, however unremunerative, trained him usefully in several fields; and his writings on the economic aspects of slavery in the pre–Civil War South won him a reputation as a social critic and acquaintance with contemporaries eminent in letters and politics. The sponsorship of some of these friends led to his appointment, in 1857, as superintendent of labor on Central Park in New York.

A trip to England in 1850 had taken Olmsted to Birkenhead Park, the new public pleasure ground near Liverpool, and the value—aesthetic, sanitary, social and economic—of a rural park to a large city had immediately aroused his intense and critical interest. Thus, when a competition was opened for a new plan for Central Park to replace the unsatisfactory one first accepted, Olmsted, with Calvert Vaux, an English architect familiar with the rural parks of England and protege and successor of Andrew Jackson Downing, devised and submitted the winning plan. In 1858 they were appointed to execute it, launching the rural park movement and the profession of landscape architecture in the United States.

Except for the Civil War period, when he became, first,

Central Park (1858–c. 1880), New York, one of Olmsted's major urban accomplishments. Romantic in style, oriented to the land and small-scale in detail, the park was planned in anticipation of the city's future open-space needs and may be considered the beginning of modern urban planning. (All, National Park Service, Frederick Law Olmsted National Historic Site)

Frederick Law Olmsted. (National Park Service, Olmsted NHS)

Plan of Riverside, Ill. (1869). The suburb consisted of lots laid out along irregularly curved streets conforming to the contour of the land. An extensive parklike common followed the course of the river.

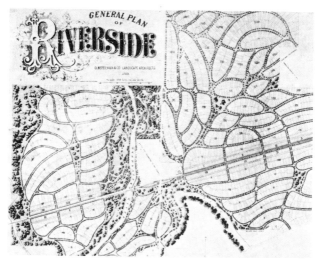

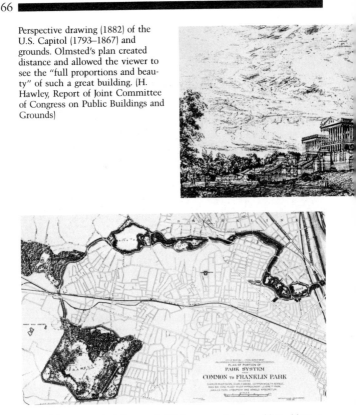

Perspective drawing (1882) of the U.S. Capitol (1793–1867) and grounds. Olmsted's plan created distance and allowed the viewer to see the "full proportions and beauty" of such a great building. (H. Hawley, Report of Joint Committee of Congress on Public Buildings and Grounds)

Plan of the Boston Park System (1896), known as the Emerald Necklace, a series of parks extending five miles from the heart of the city to the suburbs. (National Park Service, Olmsted NHS)

Opposite: World's Columbian Exposition (1893), Chicago. Olmsted's plan was classical in style, dominated by structures and monumentally scaled. (National Park Service, Olmsted NHS)

executive secretary of the U.S. Sanitary Commission, a forerunner of the Red Cross, and then manager of an ailing gold-mining property in California, Olmsted devoted himself to landscape architecture and to the movement to conserve for public enjoyment such exceptional natural scenery as Yosemite Valley and Niagara Falls. Under his leadership, treatment of landscape evolved from landscape gardening, concerned principally with the scenic improvement of the grounds of residences, public buildings and rural cemeteries, into landscape architecture, with its wider focus on the arrangement of large expanses not only for scenic effect but for the health, convenience and recreation of all classes on common ground.

Although Olmsted's nationwide practice included designs for private places, public buildings, institutions, railroad stations, military installations, suburban developments, college campuses and city squares, his reputation rests most firmly on his monumental contributions to urban amenity, such as the grounds of the U.S. Capitol, with the grand architectural terrace he proposed, and the great parks and park systems he and his associates executed for such big cities as New York, Brooklyn, Buffalo, Montreal, Detroit and Boston. He designed the grounds of the 1893 World's Columbian Exposition to be integrated, after the closing of the fair, into the existing

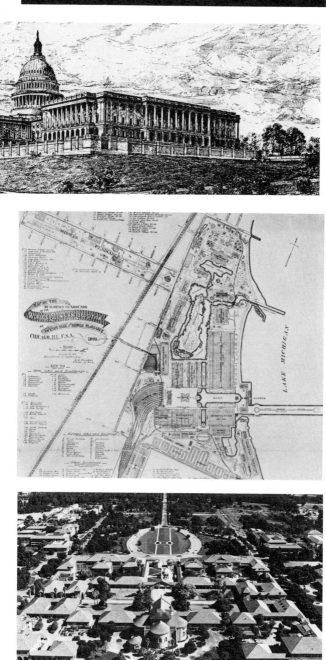

Stanford University (1887–91, Shepley, Rutan and Coolidge), Stanford, Calif., whose grounds were planned by Olmsted in a formal, symmetrical arrangement. (Stanford University)

Chicago park system he had designed 20 years before.

Olmsted's private life was remarkable only for his unremitting industry and his deep concern for the future of his profession. Because no academic training in landscape architecture existed in the 19th century, Olmsted trained in his own office many of the next generation of landscape architects, including his stepson John Charles and son Frederick Law Olmsted, Jr., who carried his ideas and ideals well into the 20th century. ◣

Plan for a Federal-style church from an early pattern book published by Asher Benjamin. (Society for the Preservation of New England Antiquities)

Cover of *Palliser's Model Homes* (1878), featuring an American version of the Eastlake style.

PATTERN BOOKS
David Gebhard

The rapid spread of American architectural fashions—the Italianate style in the 1830s and 1840s, the California bungalow in the first years of the 20th century and the California ranch house after World War II—has been due to a considerable extent to the continuous flood of pattern books that have been published and used in this country.

The forerunners of American pattern books were books written by architects and illustrated with their own designs to depict methods of design and construction. The first of these was Abraham Swan's *The British Architect*, published in America in 1775, followed by the *Collection of Designs in Architecture*. Both were reissues of volumes that had come out many years before in London. Asher Benjamin has often been credited as the first American author of pattern books, but his numerous volumes, beginning in 1797, are in essence expanded carpenter's manuals and not, strictly speaking, pattern books. From the 19th century on into the present, however, many of these carpenter's manuals have contained designs adopted widely for houses, churches and schools.

The first type of true pattern book is that published by architects, designers and plan book services whose aim has been to sell working drawings and specifications to their readers. Minard Lafever's *The Beauties of Modern Architecture* (1835) was perhaps the first architect's pattern book in America. In 1876 Palliser, Palliser and Company published *Palliser's Model Homes for the People*. The firm published a number of pattern books, including *Courthouses, Village and City Halls* (1879) and even *Memorials and Headstones* (1891). Equally prolific were the California architects Samuel and Joseph Cather Newsom, who between 1884 and 1900 wrote some 10 pattern books, from which working drawings and specifications could be ordered. In the 1920s and on into the 1930s the American Institute of Architects (with the support of Herbert Hoover as secretary of commerce and later as president) established the Architect's Small House Service Bureau. Through such pattern books as *Correctly Designed Spanish Homes* (1930) or the magazine *The*

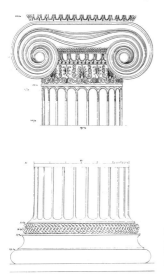

Ionic details based on one of the porticoes of the Erectheum, Athens, from Minard Lafever's *The Beauties of Modern Architecture* (1835).

Plan and elevation of a single-level Queen Anne cottage from Samuel and Joseph C. Newsom's *Picturesque California Homes* (1884–85), a house type that eventually led to the 20th-century bungalow.

Small Home (1922–32), a family could order plans and also arrange for an architect's services. Much of the influence of Royal Barry Wills, who popularized the colonial Cape Cod house in the 1930s and 1940s, and Cliff May, who popularized the California ranch house in the 1950s and 1960s, has been due to their published pattern books rather than to their completed buildings.

Beginning in the 1880s several types of pattern books also were published by home magazines such as the *Ladies' Home Journal, Good Housekeeping, Keith's Home Magazine, The Craftsman, Sunset* and many others. In some instances, the reader could order working drawings and specifications; in others, such as *Sunset Western Ranch House* (1948), edited by Cliff May, the magazine's intent was to influence middle- and upper-middle-class taste.

Another type of pattern book is intended to market specific products, ranging from plans to ready-made houses and garages. Since the late 19th century, manufacturers of prebuilt or ready-cut buildings have produced pattern book catalogs, which constitute a fascinating chapter in the history of American architecture and taste. The Sears, Roebuck and Company catalogs are examples of this type. The design of the houses offered encom-

Opposite: Stair hall from *Modern Dwellings* (1878), incorporating elements of the Eastlake and Queen Anne styles.

The "Standard" house plan from *Aladdin Homes* (1919). The four-square house was a builder's favorite from the 1890s to the 1920s.

passed the varied styles fashionable at the moment, from the late Queen Anne to the Craftsman and numerous versions of the American colonial. "It is quite likely," noted the company's 1910 *Modern Homes* catalog, "any selection you make from this book will be a house that has been built according to our plans time and time again—every architectural error or discrepancy has been overcome, therefore our plans are guaranteed foolproof." This book contained more than 80 illustrated plans for cottages and houses, plus plans for garages, barns, hog houses, corn cribs and chicken houses.

Manufacturers and manufacturers' associations also have published pattern books to encourage the use of their products: Portland Cement for concrete houses, iron or steel for metal framed and sheathed buildings, brick and hollow tile for surface and structure and prebuilt woodwork for suburban dwellings. Often, especially from 1910 through the 1920s, such pattern books were coupled with national or regional competitions that were well publicized in newspapers, popular home magazines and professional building and architectural journals.

Popular home magazines even today advertise many different types of pattern books, indicating that this source of architectural fashion is still a staple in the 1980s.

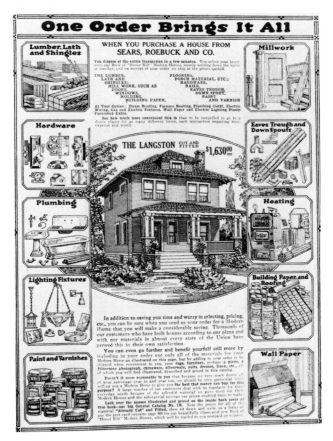

Page from Sears's "Honor Bilt" *Modern Homes* catalog, through which 20th-century homeowners could order not only houses but also everything to put in them.

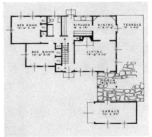

Right and below: Cape Cod "half-house" from Royal Barry Wills's *Houses for Home-makers* (1945). This simple plan allowed for fairly economical construction and the later addition of two bedrooms and a bath on the second floor.

Opposite: Cover of Lehigh Portland Cement Company's *28 Better Homes*, reflecting the 1920s interest in the romance, charm and nonurban houses of the past.

Design for casual living with Modernist overtones from Cliff May's *Sunset Western Ranch Houses* (1952).

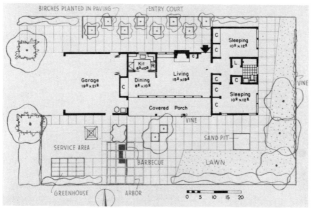

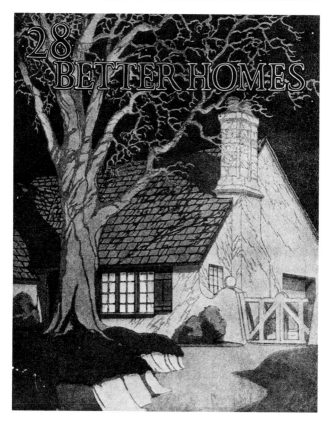

ALFRED B. MULLETT
Antoinette J. Lee

Alfred B. Mullett (1834–90) is the best known of the 15 supervising architects who administered the federal government's architecture program when it was housed in the Treasury Department. During the eight years that he served as supervising architect, Mullett designed 40 new public buildings: custom houses, federal courthouses, post offices, branch mints, appraisers' stores and assay offices. He was architect also of the State, War and Navy Building (1871–88), Washington, D.C., now the Old Executive Office Building, adjacent to the White House.

Mullett was born in Taunton, Somerset County, England. In 1844 the Mullett family settled in Glendale, a farming community on the outskirts of Cincinnati. Mullett attended Farmers College until 1854, when he left on his own accord. Two years later he joined the architectural firm headed by the well-known practitioner Isaiah Rogers, becoming a partner by 1860.

That same year Mullett struck out on his own. The following year, when the Civil War broke out, Mullett organized the Dennison, Ohio, regiment to fight for the Union cause. Ohio's quota was filled, however, and the regiment disbanded in Washington, D.C. Soon after, Mullett obtained a position as a clerk in the Treasury Department. When Rogers was appointed supervising architect in 1862, Mullett was transferred to his office as a clerk. He rose rapidly through the ranks and by Rogers's departure in 1865 was assistant supervising architect.

Mullett was appointed supervising architect in 1866 and served until 1874, presiding over the federal architecture program from the lean years of the immediate post–Civil War era to the prosperous years when nearly every city was the beneficiary of a major new federal building. Mullett's earliest designs, such as those for the San Francisco Mint (1869–74) and the Portland, Maine, Courthouse and Post Office (1866–74), were classical in

U.S. Courthouse and Post Office (1871–74), Columbia, S.C. (National Archives)

Opposite: St. Louis Post Office and Custom House (1872–84), a robust Second Empire–style building. (Robert Pettus)

Alfred B. Mullett, mid-1860s. (Courtesy Suzanne Mullett Smith)

style. His later major federal buildings, such as those for New York, Boston, Philadelphia, Cincinnati, Chicago, St. Louis and Washington, D.C., were Second Empire, a style that enjoyed considerable popularity in public building design in the 1860s and 1870s. Despite Mullett's identification with the Second Empire style, he was sensitive to the architectural traditions of smaller communities, and his designs reflected a range of styles popular during that period.

The dramatic growth of the federal architecture program proved tempting to politically influential men, especially those close to President Ulysses S. Grant's inner circle. Although Mullett was recognized as an outstanding administrator of this large construction program, he was unable to withstand pressure by key politicians to reward their home states, constituencies and friends. Mullett was further troubled by the efforts of the American Institute of Architects to open federal architecture projects to competition.

The workload made heavy demands on Mullett's health. With the appointment of Benjamin H. Bristow as secretary of the treasury in 1874, Mullett's hold on his position diminished. He resigned in late 1874.

After his government service, Mullett enjoyed a busy but not financially successful architectural career in Washington, D.C., where he designed many commercial and residential structures. For a brief period in the early 1880s, he was in partnership with the architects William G. Steinmetz and Hugo Kafka in New York. His failure to collect professional fees for his work on the State, War and Navy Building and private work sent his health into further decline. He died in 1890 of a self-inflicted bullet wound.

Despite his professional difficulties, Mullett will be remembered as the head of the largest "architectural office" of the Gilded Age and the first American architect to achieve a professional reputation that reached from coast to coast. ◢

U.S. Branch Mint (1869–74), San Francisco, a Greek Revival building that withstood the earthquake of 1906. (National Archives)

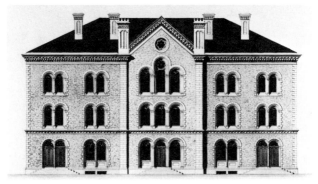

U.S. Custom House (1867–73), St. Paul, Minn., showing Mullett's adaptation of the Romanesque style to a "territorial" setting. (National Archives)

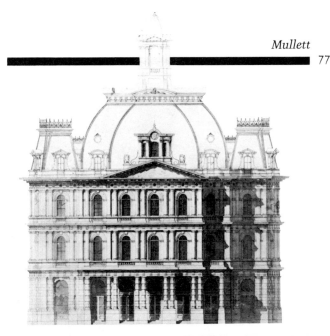

U.S. Post Office and Courthouse (1869–75). New York, one of Mullett's earliest public buildings in the Second Empire style. (National Archives)

Apex Building (1888), Washington, D.C. Mullett designed the brownstone facade and two corner turrets of this office building. (© 1984 Carol M. Highsmith)

Frieze of the main cornice in the customs room, U.S. Custom House (1866–74), Portland, Maine. (National Archives)

Old Executive Office Building (State, War and Navy Building) (1871–88), Washington, D.C., one of the grandest surviving Second Empire–style buildings in the United States. (National Archives)

H. H. Richardson, in 1879 and around 1883. (Society for the Preservation of New England Antiquities; George Collins Cox, Courtesy Joseph P. Richardson)

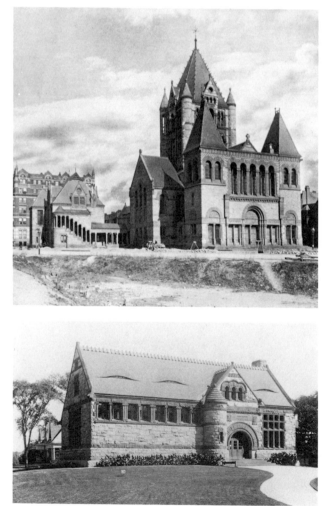

Middle: Trinity Church (1872–77), Boston, a unified composition including a parish house. (SPNEA)

Crane Library (1880–82), Quincy, Mass., the masterpiece of Richardson's libraries. (SPNEA)

HENRY HOBSON RICHARDSON
Jeffrey Karl Ochsner

Henry Hobson Richardson (1838–86) transformed the course of American architecture—indeed, some historians have acclaimed him America's greatest 19th-century architect—and then died at the height of his career. His influence was immense: His buildings were the basis for a decade of Romanesque Revival architecture in America; his best designs were the inspiration for the innovative architects of the Chicago School; and his assistants included many of the leaders of the next generation of American architects, including Charles McKim, Stanford White, George Shepley and John Galen Howard.

Born and raised in Louisiana, Richardson was graduated from Harvard College in 1859 and attended the Ecole des Beaux-Arts in Paris after 1860. He returned to the United States in 1865 and opened his professional practice in New York in 1866. That November he won his first commission, for Unity Church (1866–68), Springfield, Mass.

In 1867 Richardson entered into partnership with Charles Dexter Gambrill, who acted as business manager for the firm. Richardson's early buildings followed the then-current Gothic and Second Empire styles. In a series of commissions beginning about 1870, however, Richardson began to explore designs with forms derived from Romanesque sources. Projects such as Brattle Square Church (1869–73), Boston, and the New York State Hospital (1869–80), Buffalo, led to his successful entry in the 1872 competition for Trinity Church, Boston. The publicity about Trinity Church, particularly after its completion in 1877, propelled him to the front rank of American architects.

In 1878 Richardson dissolved the partnership and moved his office to Brookline, Mass. Over the next eight years he refined his mature style through the simplification of form and the elimination of extraneous ornament and historical detail. Among the notable projects from this phase of his career are his buildings at Harvard University, Sever Hall (1878–80) and Austin Hall (1881–84); a series of small libraries, primarily those in the Boston suburbs of Woburn, North Easton, Quincy and Malden; and a series of railroad stations, including nine for the Boston and Albany Railroad Company. In addition, Richardson designed several commercial structures, such as the Cheney Building (1875–76), Hartford, and three stores in Boston for the Ames family. He also collaborated on the design for the New York State Capitol (1876–86), Albany, and was responsible for the dramatic Senate Chamber, western stair and multiple judicial and executive chambers.

Richardson's houses were marked by significant departures in domestic design. His initial exploration of living hall planning culminated in the William Watts Sherman House (1874–76), Newport, the first Queen Anne design in America. His later country houses, beginning with the Dr. John Bryant House (1880–81), Cohasset, Mass., further developed living hall planning and represented a critical phase of the mature Shingle Style. Richardson's urban houses, usually of brick or stone, also took advantage of the planning innovations of his country houses; among

Sever Hall (1878–80), Harvard University, Cambridge, Mass., designed to fit the context of Harvard Yard's existing buildings of different periods and styles. (SPNEA)

Old Colony Railroad Station (1881–84), North Easton, Mass., a granite building with brownstone trim, originally with long passenger sheds. (Boston Atheneum)

the most important were the John Hay and Henry Adams houses (1884–86), Washington, D.C., and the J. J. Glessner House (1885–87), Chicago.

Richardson's career culminated in the design of the Allegheny County Courthouse and Jail (1883–88), Pittsburgh, and the Marshall Field Wholesale Store (1885–87), Chicago. These structures epitomized the growing sense of gravity, sobriety and stateliness that is the hallmark of his best work.

Richardson's health was never particularly good, and, beseiged with commissions later in his career, he practiced at a hectic pace. Richardson died at the age of 47 in 1886. His office was continued under the name Shepley, Rutan and Coolidge by his three chief assistants, who saw that his remaining buildings were completed as he had intended. ▷

Mrs. Mary Fisk Stoughton House (1882–83), Cambridge, Mass., considered one of Richardson's finest examples of domestic architecture. (George W. Sheldon, *Artistic Country Seats*)

J. J. Glessner House (1885–87), Chicago, built of rock-faced granite with an interior court. (Eric N. DeLony, HABS)

Marshall Field Wholesale Store (1885–87), Chicago, one of Richardson's most famous buildings. The windows above the first floor were grouped under arches in a rhythm that doubled and then quadrupled on the higher floors. (Chicago Historical Society)

Top and above: Allegheny County Courthouse and Jail (1883–88),
Pittsburgh, a sophisticated design resolution of complex functional
requirements. The jail, in the shape of an asymmetrical cross, is connected
to the courthouse by the Bridge of Sighs. (Both, Houghton Library, Harvard
University)

Albany City Hall (1880–83), Albany, N.Y. The front entrance is marked by a triple compound arch. (Stephen Brown)

Senate Chamber, New York State Capitol (1876–86), Albany, designed by Richardson and Stanford White. The room is more than 50 feet high and has an oak ceiling. (Mendel, Mesick, Cohen, Waite, Hall Architects)

FRANK FURNESS
James F. O'Gorman

Son of the noted literary figure and Unitarian minister
William Henry Furness, Frank Furness (1839–1912) was
born into a prominent Philadelphia family that was
intellectual as well as artistic. He began his architectural
training in New York in the 1850s under French-educated
Richard Morris Hunt and fully intended to continue his
studies in Paris until the Civil War interrupted his career.
His family was abolitionist, and he fought as a cavalry
officer for three years with such fervor that in 1899 he
was awarded the Congressional Medal of Honor for
bravery under fire at Trevilian Station, Va., in 1864.
Furness is the sole American architect of note to receive
his country's highest military decoration.

Returning to Philadelphia after his discharge, he began
a colorful career that was to carry him to the top of his
profession. In partnership with John Fraser and George W.
Hewitt, he designed the Pennsylvania Academy of the
Fine Arts (1871–76), Philadelphia, a Second Empire–style
composition enriched with Victorian Gothic details. This
was an era of English and French influence in American
building, and this first major work heralded Furness as an
outstanding practitioner of the picturesque eclectic style
in which buildings were designed by the accumulation of
discordant details, colors, textures and ornament imported
from overseas.

The 1870s and 1880s saw one building after another
issue from Furness's drafting board, each more powerful

Frank Furness, 1906. (James C. Massey Collection)

Above and right: Pennsylvania Academy of the Fine Arts (1871–76), Philadelphia. The exterior and interior display exuberant and detailed ornamentation. (Gutekunst, Pennsylvania Academy of the Fine Arts Archives; Carleton Knight III)

and aggressive than the other. The Provident Life and Trust Company Building (1876–79), Philadelphia, epitomized his style, with its oversized details squeezed onto a narrow front and its high, bright and colorful banking room beyond a menacing portal. Although he continued to practice, in partnership with Allen Evans, until near his death, Furness's design career culminated with the Library (now the Furness Building) at the University of Pennsylvania (1887–91), Philadelphia. Here picturesque eclecticism achieved its apogee, with an anthology of details from the whole history of architecture piled into an asymmetrical mass of red brick and terra cotta ornament. It was at once Furness's masterpiece and his swan song, as the emergent classicism announced by McKim, Mead and White's contemporary Boston Public Library was to carry the immediate future.

A major figure in post–Civil War Philadelphia architecture, designing buildings of all types for city and suburb, Furness was largely forgotten by the time of his death. His impact was to emerge only in the 1960s and 1970s when successors such as Robert Venturi, reacting to the sameness of the International Style, found in his work the excitement and richness they sought in Post-Modern design. It was then that Furness assumed his rightful place among America's most formative architects. ▨

Furness Building (Library) (1887–91), University of Pennsylvania, Philadelphia, the culmination of Furness's eclecticism with details taken from the spectrum of architectural history. (James C. Massey Collection)

First Unitarian Church (1885–86), Philadelphia, before the removal of the entrance porch. (James C. Massey Collection)

Pennsylvania Railroad (Broad Street) Station (1881–82), Philadelphia, distinguished by terra cotta reliefs, an immense train shed and a castlelike tower. (James C. Massey Collection)

Opposite: William Preston House (c. 1885), Philadelphia, which seemed large but was built on a small city lot. *(Inland Architect)*

Guarantee Trust and Safe Deposit Company (1873–75), Philadelphia, flaunting overscaled details. (Historical Society of Pennsylvania)

RICHARD MORRIS HUNT
Paul R. Baker

Often called the dean of American architecture, Richard Morris Hunt (1827–95) was, toward the close of the 19th century, the best known and most fashionable American architect. His designs ranged widely in style and in building types, although he became most famous for his sumptuous private houses. Hunt played an important role in early American architectural education. As a founder, first secretary and third president of the American Institute of Architects and spokesman for his fellow architects, Hunt probably did more than anyone else to advance the developing profession in the United States.

Born in Brattleboro, Vt., the son of a prosperous lawyer and congressman, Hunt entered the Ecole des Beaux-Arts in Paris in 1846, the first American to study there. Working in the atelier of Hector Martin Lefuel, he later collaborated with Lefuel on the Pavillon de la Bibliotheque (1854–55) of the Louvre. In 1855 Hunt settled in New York; knowledgeable, energetic and self-assured, he committed himself to attempt to raise the standards of American building design.

His Tenth Street Studio Building (1858) in New York was the earliest American structure erected specifically for artists; here he set up an atelier giving architectural instruction. His first New York town house (1857), for Thomas P. Rossiter, a painter, brought him into litigation over fees; the court case was significant in helping establish fixed charges for professional architectural services. Following his marriage in 1861, Hunt revisited France, the first of several long return sojourns in Europe.

During the late 1860s and the 1870s, Hunt's work included numerous domestic buildings in Newport, New York, Chicago and Boston. In New York he also designed the large Presbyterian Hospital (1872) and the nearby Lenox Library (1877), two iron-front stores (1872–74), the Tribune Building (1876), for a time the tallest commercial building in the city, and the Stuyvesant (1870), the earliest important American multifamily residence.

Several 1880s commissions were for the wealthy Vanderbilt family, including St. Mark's Church (1880), Islip, N.Y.; a huge mausoleum (1889) on Staten Island; the Jackson Square Branch of the New York Free Circulating Library (1887), a small Flemish-style building; and the much-admired chateaulike William K. Vanderbilt Mansion (1882), New York. Hunt often collaborated with the sculptor John Quincy Adams Ward, as on the Washington Statue (1883), New York, and the Yorktown Monument (1884), Yorktown, Va. His most important monumental work was the base and pedestal for the Statue of Liberty, dedicated in 1886.

From the mid-1880s Hunt designed several mansions. In Newport he created the Busk House (1891), on a rocky coastal site; Ochre Court (1892), with French Gothic and early Renaissance elements; Marble House (1892), a neoclassical structure with luxurious interiors; Belcourt Castle (1894), in an eclectic style; and The Breakers (1895), a 70-room cottage in a Genoese style. The most splendid of Hunt's mansions, Biltmore House (1895), a 225-room chateau, was created for George W. Vanderbilt in Asheville, N.C., on 125,000 acres of grounds.

Richard Morris Hunt. (James Garrison, American Institute of Architects Foundation)

Biltmore House (1895), Asheville, N.C., a French Renaissance-style mansion considered the largest private house in the United States. Frederick Law Olmsted landscaped the grounds. (Biltmore House)

Marble House (1892), Newport, R.I. The splendid dining room reflects the lavishness of the mansion. (Preservation Society of Newport County)

Heading the board of architects for the 1893 World's Columbian Exposition, Hunt designed the Administration Building, the fair's dominating architectural feature. Work for Harvard University and the U.S. Military Academy added to his several earlier academic commissions at Yale and Princeton universities and elsewhere. His final commission was the monumental entrance wing (1895) for New York's Metropolitan Museum of Art.

After Hunt's death in 1895, several art associations erected a Hunt Memorial in New York. Dedicated in 1898, the memorial remains a striking tribute to one who did so much for American architecture. ◣

Administration Building and North Ward Pavilion, Presbyterian Hospital
(1872), New York, incorporating new concepts of hospital design. (Museum
of the City of New York)

The Stuyvesant (1869), New York,
the first apartment building in the
United States, with four units per
floor. (Museum of the City of New
York)

Statue of Liberty (Frederic Bartholdi, 1886), New York, for which Hunt designed the base and pedestal, ornamented with neo-Greek details. (AIA Foundation)

Entrance wing (1895–1902), Metropolitan Museum of Art, New York, an example of the ornate Beaux-Arts style. (Museum of the City of New York)

Court of Honor, World's Columbian Exposition, Chicago, view from east to west, with Hunt's Administration Building (1893) at the end of the reflecting pool. (Chicago Historical Society)

William Rutherford Mead, Charles Follen McKim and Stanford White,
c. 1905. (Avery Architectural and Fine Arts Library)

McKIM, MEAD AND WHITE
Leland M. Roth

This highly respected and enormously busy architectural firm, based in New York, began in 1874 when Charles Follen McKim (1847–1909) and William Rutherford Mead (1846–1928) began to collaborate in their work; in 1879 they joined with Stanford White (1853–1906), and the firm was established. Through their widely different but complementary personalities—McKim was a conservative traditionalist and White was an adventurous artist—and their many connections in the worlds of art, literature, business and politics, they attracted a broad spectrum of clients, resulting in nearly 1,000 building commissions. Their office was the largest in the world, employing as many as 80 to 100 people and functioning also as an atelier through which passed many young architects who became leaders of their profession in the 20th century.

Mead studied at Amherst College before working for the architect Russell Sturgis and then pursuing independent study in Florence. McKim, the son of an ardent abolitionist leader, was raised in eastern Pennsylvania and studied for a year at the Lawrence Scientific School of Harvard University before studying for three years at the Ecole des Beaux-Arts in Paris. White, a native of New York and the son of a prominent literary and art critic, was a skilled self-trained draftsman and watercolorist who was apprenticed in H. H. Richardson's office, where McKim was also employed following his studies in Paris.

The young architects rose to prominence designing country retreats in Newport, R.I., such as the Newport Casino (1879–81) and the Isaac Bell House (1881–83). Their drive toward an ever more elemental form culminated in the William G. Low House (1886–87), which had the form of a single broad triangular gable. The partners were also designing urban townhouses, of which the best were the Villard Houses (1882–85), New York, a

Opposite: Newport Casino (1879–81), Newport, R.I., which marked the beginning of the Shingle Style. (Rhode Island Historical Society)

William G. Low House (1886–87), Bristol, R.I., representing the apogee of the Shingle Style with its geometric form. (Cervin Robinson, HABS)

Villard Houses (1882–85), New York, six private houses with restrained
Renaissance details, arranged in a U-shape around a court. (Museum of the
City of New York)

King Model Houses (1891–92),
New York, a three-block area in
Harlem developed by David H.
King to house middle-income fami-
lies. (Leland M. Roth)

Henry A. C. Taylor House
(1885–86), Newport, R.I. Based on
18th-century Newport houses, it
inaugurated the Colonial Revival
style. (Leland M. Roth Collection)

Boston Public Library (1887–95), which set the pattern for public libraries
for more than 50 years. (Society for the Preservation of New England
Antiquities)

group of six arranged around a central court and based on Renaissance sources.

As a result of these early successes, the firm was appointed to design the Boston Public Library (1887–95), the largest public lending institution in the world. It was restrained in external character, forming a sedate wall for the space of Copley Square, yet resplendent internally with the embellishments of many sculptors and painters, in the best tradition of the Ecole. The same union of the arts in the service of public education was evident in the smaller Walker Art Gallery (1891–94) at Bowdoin College, Brunswick, Maine. For more lighthearted public functions the firm designed the festive Madison Square Garden (1887–90), New York.

The architects participated in the World's Columbian Exposition in Chicago, designing the Agriculture Building (1890–93). This work influenced McKim's master plan for the new campus of Columbia University and White's plan for the new campus of New York University. As a result of this planning activity, McKim was asked by Daniel H. Burnham to serve on the Senate Park Commission to replan the District of Columbia in 1902.

The firm concluded its career with a flourish of imposing public buildings that have remained models of their type, including the Knickerbocker Trust (1901–04), New York; the J. P. Morgan Library (1902–07), New York; the Rhode Island State Capitol (1891–1903), Providence; the addition to the Bank of Montreal (1900–05), Montreal; and the expansion of the Metropolitan Museum of Art (1904–20), New York. Perhaps the firm's finest achievement was Pennsylvania Station (1902–10), the vast New York terminal for the Pennsylvania Railroad, in which the architects successfully handled the many conflicting functional demands of long-distance and commuting traffic, creating a building that served as a monumental gateway to the city. McKim, Mead and White also designed many diverse works including two electrical generating stations, a textile factory, workers' housing in two new industrial towns and a broad spectrum of public buildings for small, industrial Naugatuck, Conn., during the period 1891–1905, including two public schools and a public library. The firm also handled the reconstruction (1896–99) of the Rotunda of the University of Virginia, Charlottesville, after a disastrous fire. In 1909 McKim received the American Institute of Architect's Gold Medal.

McKim, Mead and White attempted to create an American urban architecture suited to American urban life but did so in the light of American architectural traditions, which to them meant the Georgian decorum of the nation's first cities—Boston, Salem, old New York and Philadelphia. The firm adopted classicism but exercised a discriminating eclecticism that adhered to Renaissance, Georgian and austere Roman sources. McKim's formal training and innate sobriety provided clarity of form to which White added richness of texture and plasticity in ornamentation. Working within the conventions of 19th-century idealist formalism with its allusions to the architecture of the past, McKim, Mead and White represented the most generous realization of the triad of commodious planning, sound construction and visual delight first propounded by the Roman writer on architecture Vitruvius in the first century B.C. ◪

Rhode Island State Capitol (1891–1903), Providence, a white marble building that was a model for state capitol buildings until 1935. (RIHS)

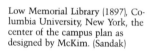

Low Memorial Library (1897), Columbia University, New York, the center of the campus plan as designed by McKim. (Sandak)

Pennsylvania Station (1902–10), New York, a grand station based on the Baths of Caracalla with a monumental steel and glass concourse. (Pennsylvania Railroad)

Madison Square Garden (1887–91), New York. This multipurpose building contained a huge amphitheater, two theaters, a restaurant and a roof garden where White was shot while attending a cabaret. (New-York Historical Society)

WILLIAM LE BARON JENNEY
Theodore Turak

William Le Baron Jenney (1832–1907) was a park and town planner, an innovator in building technology and a teacher. Born into a family of whaling ship owners in Fairhaven, Mass., he received a practical education at Phillips Academy, Andover, and other New England schools. After a voyage to the South Pacific he entered the Lawrence Scientific School of Harvard University to study civil engineering, but finding the instruction inadequate he transferred to the Ecole Centrale des Arts et Manufactures, Paris, studying there from 1853 to 1856. There he learned the latest iron construction techniques as well as the classical functionalist doctrine of J. N. L. Durand, the standard architectural curriculum of French engineering schools.

He returned to Paris after working in Mexico and decided to become an architect. Service as an engineering officer in the Civil War intervened, but by 1868 he had begun his career in Chicago. In 1876–77 he held the first professorship of architecture at the University of Michigan.

The West Parks were among his first commissions in Chicago. Inspired by Baron Haussmann's plan for the renewal of Paris, he created a system of major parks— Humboldt, Garfield and Douglas—and minor parks connected by grand, tree-lined boulevards. At the same time he collaborated with Olmsted and Vaux in the planning of Riverside, Ill., where he also designed homes and several important larger buildings.

His domestic work was characterized by houses possessing free and open ground plans, such as the Col. James H. Bowen House (1868), Hyde Park, Ill., and equipped with the latest in technical conveniences. The styles followed the general eclecticism of the era,

West Parks (1870s), Chicago. Jenney's tree-lined boulevards, rather than being slashing diagonals, followed the existing street grid; small, informal, English-style parks were located at each right angle. (Chicago Park Reports)

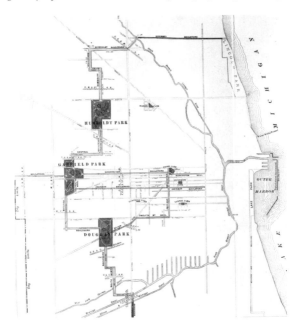

William Le Baron Jenney. (Hesler, Chicago Historical Society)

Col. James H. Bowen House (1868), Hyde Park, Ill., a Swiss chalet with open circulation that predates Frank Lloyd Wright's early work. (Jenney, *Principles and Practices of Architecture,* 1869)

although his expressed preference was for a modern Gothic.

Jenney's fame rests mainly on his commercial buildings in Chicago. The first Leiter Building (1879) was virtually a glass box. Iron columns backed exterior masonry piers, thus permitting greater window areas; otherwise, its construction was conventional. In the nine-and-one-half-story Home Insurance Building (1884–85), Jenney brought together the most advanced technologies to create the prototype of the skyscraper supported by a metal skeleton. He extended the interior fireproofed frame to the exterior by inserting iron columns into the brick piers.

Using iron supports and steel beams in his second Leiter Building (now the Sears, Roebuck Building) (1889–91), Jenney opened the walls to an unprecedented degree. The severe cubic quality of the elevation recalls the teachings of Durand while predicting the principles of the Bauhaus. Jenney achieved the first 16-story skeleton-frame office building in the Manhattan Building (1889–91), but certainly the most elegant expression of his principles was the Ludington Building (1891). Jenney helped promote the World's Columbian Exposition held in Chicago in 1893 and designed its Horticultural Building. Considered one of the fair's finest structures, its area of five and one-quarter acres made it the largest botanical conservatory built at that time.

Jenney read James Fergusson, Viollet-le-Duc and other important architectural writers of his century, synthesizing their ideas and passing them on to his student draftsmen. Since these included some of the most eminent architects of the 19th century, such as Daniel H. Burnham and Louis Sullivan, it can be said that he was the founder of the Chicago School of architecture. ◬

Second Leiter Building (1889–91), Chicago, whose clear, simple functionalism anticipated the aesthetic of the Bauhaus. (Chicago Architectural Photographing Company, David R. Phillips)

Ludington Building (1891), Chicago, built of steel construction to bear the weight of a publishing company's printing presses. Renaissance motifs decorate the terra cotta sheathing. (Art Institute of Chicago)

Home Insurance Building (1884–85), Chicago, a fireproof masonry building supported by an iron frame. (Chicago Historical Society)

Manhattan Building (1889–91), Chicago. Flanking side bays are supported on cantilevers anchored in the building's core, and the setback anticipates skyscrapers of the 1930s. (Chicago Historical Society)

Horticultural Building (1893), World's Columbian Exposition, Chicago. Its iron and glass dome was illuminated from the interior by electric lights. (Chicago Historical Society)

BURNHAM AND ROOT
Thomas S. Hines

Daniel Hudson Burnham (1846–1912) and John Wellborn Root (1850–91) were partners in a firm that, along with William Le Baron Jenney, Adler and Sullivan, and Holabird and Roche, shaped and led the Chicago School of skyscraper architecture. Root was born in Lumpkin, Ga. Burnham was born in Henderson, N.Y., but grew up in Chicago. Of the two, Root had a better formal education, with preparatory schooling in Liverpool, England, and a degree in civil engineering from New York University. Burnham's scholarship was less impressive than his social, artistic and managerial talents, and he was rejected by both Harvard and Yale universities. Yet, his drawing skill was sufficient to get him work in Jenney's office and later in the firm of Peter B. Wight, both busily engaged in rebuilding Chicago after the fire of 1871. In Wight's office, Burnham met John Root, and the two formed a partnership in 1873.

Both men sensed the differing but reciprocal qualities of talent and temperament that, when integrated, would form the ideal partnership. Amiable, quick-witted and brilliant among friends, Root was shy and reserved in public. Unless guided and stimulated, he also tended to procrastinate. Burnham, on the other hand, toughened by his earlier failures, had grown increasingly determined, aggressive and persuasive and ultimately became the chief office administrator and liaison with clients. He was also, Root acknowledged, mainly responsible for the planning and layout of most of the firm's buildings and served as a perceptive critic of the architectural designs, which both partners considered Root's special domain.

During their 18-year partnership, Burnham and Root built hotels, railway stations, stores, warehouses, schools, hospitals, churches and more than 200 private residences and apartment buildings. Yet, their greatest achievements were the tall office buildings that would come to be called skyscrapers.

Although Burnham and Root built numerous metal-cage, steel-framed buildings in the late 1880s and 1890s, their most famous skyscrapers, ironically, were three wall-bearing structures, all built in Chicago for the developers Peter and Shepherd Brooks. The 10-story Montauk Block (1881–82) was virtually without traditional historical references, predicting in its stern obeisance to functionalism much of the ethic and aesthetic of the subsequent Modern movement. The Rookery (1885–87) was a more consciously elaborate building with Root's lush ornament highlighting the Romanesque stylistic references. Its logical internal plan, attributed to Burnham, with four connecting wings surrounding a light court, would long serve as a model for skyscraper layout. The stark, dark Monadnock Building (1889–91) divested itself of ornament even more explicitly than the Montauk. Despite the anachronism, demanded by the client, of its dramatically flared, wall-bearing structure, the Monadnock would become another canonical monument of Modernism. The Mills Building (1890–91), San Francisco, reflected a significant synthesis of the essential skyscraper elements: steel frame, four-winged plan around a central light court and orderly Chicago School propor-

Daniel H. Burnham, c. 1880. (Art Institute of Chicago)

John Root, c. 1880. (Art Institute of Chicago)

Montauk Block (1881–82), Chicago, an austere, structurally innovative design that predicted the new "functionalist" aesthetic. (Art Institute of Chicago)

Montezuma Hotel (1883–85), Las Vegas, N.M., a rustic retreat built of shingles, wood and sandstone. When constructed, it was the only hotel in the United States lighted entirely by electricity. (Colorado Historical Society)

tions, as accented by Root's exuberant ornament.

Before Root's premature death in 1891, the firm had made preliminary plans for the elegant Reliance Building, also in Chicago, which Burnham completed with Charles Atwood in 1894. Burnham was also left to choreograph the epochal World's Columbian Exposition of 1893 and to pilot the firm, reconstituted as D. H. Burnham and Company. Burnham's work over the next 20 years would make continuing contributions to architecture and urban planning. His grand vision and interest in the classical revival gave impetus to the City Beautiful movement, whose principles were reflected in the 1902 plan for the renewal of the Mall area of Washington, D.C., and in the city plans for Cleveland (1903), San Francisco (1905) and Manila (1905). Yet, Burnham never found a replacement for Root in what had indeed been an ideal partnership. ◢

Top and above: The Rookery (1885–87), Chicago, featuring Romanesque detailing adapted to the large office building. Fanciful rooks and "Moorish" ornamentation adorn the rough granite arched entrance. (Both, Continental Bank, Chicago)

Reliance Building (1891–94), Chicago, which capitalized on a steel skeletal frame to display large areas of glass. (HABS; Cervin Robinson, HABS)

Mills Building (1890–91), San Francisco, a steel-framed building integrating form and function. (Gabriel Moulin, California Historical Society)

Monadnock Building (1889–91), Chicago. Despite the wall-bearing structure, the building's elegant austerity had a great influence on skyscraper design. (Hedrich-Blessing)

Plan of Washington, D.C. (1902), designed by Burnham "in a manner and to the extent commensurate with the dignity and the resources of the American Nation." The final plan reiterated and enlarged L'Enfant's plan of 1791. (Report of the Senate Committee, U.S. Commission of Fine Arts)

Louis Sullivan, at Ocean Springs, Miss.

Dankmar Adler. (Art Institute of Chicago)

ADLER AND SULLIVAN
Paul E. Sprague

During its 12 years of existence (1883–95), the Chicago firm of Adler and Sullivan left an imprint on architecture far beyond the American Midwest. Dankmar Adler (1844–1900) led the movement to license architects, with the result that the first registration act was passed in Illinois in 1897. Louis Henri Sullivan (1856–1924) became the first American architect to produce a modern style of architecture and the first architect anywhere to give aesthetic unity to the tall building.

Adler, born in Germany, emigrated with his parents first to Detroit and then to Chicago. After training in architectural offices in both cities, he became a practicing architect in Chicago during the 1870s. Sullivan joined him in 1882 as a minor partner. Full partnership came in 1883, when Adler and Sullivan was founded. Adler's father was the rabbi of an important Chicago congregation, and many of the firm's clients came from the Jewish community in Chicago.

Born in Boston, Sullivan was the son of artistic parents and was drawn to the arts at a young age. His formal education was restricted to one year in architecture at the Massachusetts Institute of Technology and another year in Paris at the Ecole des Beaux-Arts. Work in architectural offices in Philadelphia and New York provided the finishing touches.

Sullivan early on articulated a goal of creating a modern style of architecture, aspiring to design buildings that were largely original in form and detail instead of depending on historic styles for inspiration. The results of his ambition are illustrated in two structures begun in 1890: a mausoleum for the Henry Getty family in Chicago and the Wainwright Building, a tall steel-frame office building for Ellis Wainwright in St. Louis. These buildings embody masses, forms and shapes of unusual and original design and display an equally modern style of ornament as well. This ornamentation would later be viewed with disdain by many architects who converted

Stock Exchange Building (1893–94), Chicago. The horizontal character of the metal frame balances the vertically oriented bay windows. (*Inland Architect*)

Getty Tomb (1890–91), Chicago. Sullivan's first mature work in his modern style combines a simplified cubic mass with conventional floral ornament. (Paul E. Sprague)

Elevation and detail of the Wainwright Building (1886–90), St. Louis, whose bold piers emphasize the building's verticality. The cornice and recessed spandrels are decorated with ornate terra cotta. (*Inland Architect*; Paul E. Sprague)

Schlesinger and Mayer (Carson, Pirie, Scott) Building (1898–1904), Chicago, one of Sullivan's most admired designs, combining a rational plan and structure with a romantic filigree of cast-iron ornament. (Art Institute of Chicago)

Merchants' (Poweshiek County) National Bank (1914), Grinnell, Iowa, a small, late work reflecting Sullivan's continuing stylistic evolution. (Robert Thall, HABS)

Opposite: Auditorium Building (1886–90), Chicago, reflecting Sullivan's early simplification of massing. (Hedrich-Blessing)

James Charnley House (1891–91), Chicago, a splendid low-rise design showing the influence of Frank Lloyd Wright. (*Inland Architect*)

the idea of a modern style into a style that had no ornament.

For the Wainwright Building, Sullivan devised a scheme for unifying the fronts of a building that was taller than it was wide. By abandoning historic styles, most of which had been developed for buildings that were wider than tall, Sullivan was free to manipulate his materials in an original way that achieved aesthetic unity. This he achieved in the Wainwright by knitting together thin, vertical piers and textured, horizontal spandrels into an integrated architectural fabric.

Adler made these designs possible by his efficient and forward-looking management of the firm's business affairs, for he secured the clients and encouraged them to build Sullivan's unusual designs. He also took charge of the mechanical and structural aspects of design. Together they worked as an effective design team that produced numerous architectural milestones, especially between 1888 and 1895, including the Auditorium Building (1886–90), the Getty Tomb (1890–91), the Schiller Building (1891–93) and the Stock Exchange Building (1893–94), all in Chicago, and the Wainwright Building (1890–91), in St. Louis. Without Adler, it is unlikely that Sullivan could have achieved what he did; without Sullivan, Adler would probably be virtually unknown today. Yet, in 1895 they dissolved their partnership for reasons still not fully explained.

In the following years, neither architect received many commissions. Adler died in 1900, but Sullivan lived until 1924. During those years Sullivan built few buildings, yet what he built—mostly commercial buildings and banks—continued the evolution of his modern style. At the same time he explained his ideas and goals in a series of books—*Kindergarten Chats and Other Writings* (revised 1918), *Democracy: A Man Search*, never published, *The Autobiography of an Idea* (1924) and *A System of Architectural Ornament According to a Philosophy of Man's Powers* (1924). One lasting contribution of his style was that it provided the basis for the modern architectural idiom developed by his student Frank Lloyd Wright. In 1944 the American Institute of Architects awarded Sullivan its Gold Medal. ◣

CASS GILBERT
Patricia Murphy

Best known as an East Coast practitioner of the Beaux-Arts style from 1900 to 1930, Cass Gilbert (1859–1934) was born in Zanesville, Ohio, and came to St. Paul with his family in 1868. Gilbert began his architectural career working for a St. Paul architect, Abraham Radcliff, and then studied architecture for one year at the Massachusetts Institute of Technology. On his return from a European tour in 1880, Gilbert was hired by McKim, Mead and White and worked in the firm's New York office until 1882, when he was sent to Baltimore to supervise several projects.

In 1883 he returned to St. Paul, where he was one of the first professionally trained architects, and soon was designing depots, hospitals and other buildings for the Northern Pacific Railway, some in conjunction with McKim, Mead and White. From 1884 to 1892 Gilbert was in partnership with James Knox Taylor, a fellow MIT classmate, and the firm quickly became popular locally.

During the 1880s and 1890s Gilbert's work included houses, office buildings, warehouses, retail stores, churches and clubhouses. Many of his imaginative and picturesque designs recalled and reinterpreted details of European buildings seen on his Grand Tour and typified the popular styles of the era: Richardsonian Romanesque, Shingle Style, colonial revival and renditions of medieval and Renaissance styles. Gilbert's early work attracted the attention of prominent architects in New York and Chicago, including Daniel H. Burnham, and he was chosen to serve on the national jury to select architects for the 1893 World's Columbian Exposition in Chicago.

Gilbert's winning entry in the competition for the Minnesota State Capitol (1895–1905), St. Paul, led him to a prominent New York career designing monumental Beaux-Arts buildings. His design was an elegant, Renaissance-inspired masterpiece with a dome reminiscent of St. Peter's in Rome; paintings, murals and sculptures were executed by a host of nationally prominent artists.

Several commissions on the East Coast were soon

Bethlehem Presbyterian Church (1890), St. Paul, an eclectic early work. (*American Architect and Building News*, 1891)

Cass Gilbert, 1907. (Minnesota Historical Society)

awarded, the first in Boston for the Brazier Building (1896), a steel frame, Renaissance-style office block. In 1899 Gilbert won the competition to design the U.S. Custom House in New York, winning over his mentors, McKim, Mead and White, and others, and in 1910 he was selected by F. W. Woolworth to design the Woolworth Building, the tallest building in the world when it was completed in 1913.

Gilbert received commissions to design two other state capitols—the Arkansas State Capitol (1900–1917, with George R. Mann), Little Rock, and the West Virginia State Capitol (1924–32), Charleston—and other public buildings mostly in the Beaux-Arts style, some incorporating colonial revival elements. Other works included the Union Club (1902), New York, modeled after a Renaissance palazzo, the U.S. Treasury Annex (1918–19), Washington, D.C., and the public libraries of St. Louis and Hartford (both 1908) and Detroit (1921). His Palace of Fine Arts, built as part of the 1904 Louisiana Purchase Exposition, later became the St. Louis Art Museum. He executed elaborate plans for the University of Minnesota (1908), Minneapolis; the University of Texas (1910), Austin; and Oberlin College (1912), Oberlin, Ohio. The U.S. Supreme Court Building (1928–35), Washington, D.C., was completed after Gilbert's death by his son, Cass Gilbert, Jr.

Gilbert was one of several architects who founded the Architectural League of New York in 1881, and he served as its president in 1913 and 1914. He was also the president of the American Institute of Architects (1908–09) and the National Academy of Design (1926–33) and was a member of the U.S. Commission of Fine Arts from its founding in 1910 until 1916. He died on a trip to England in 1934.

Gilbert was prolific, prominent and successful and left his mark on the architecture of many American cities. Although his early work in Minnesota includes many imaginative and picturesque designs, by the early 20th century he can perhaps best be classified as an old-school, East Coast establishment architect whose academically correct and convincing designs were firmly rooted in the American Beaux-Arts tradition. ◪

Minnesota State Capitol (1895–1905), St. Paul, an elegant Beaux-Arts building that put Minnesota on the architectural map at a time when midwestern architecture was considered provincial. (Minnesota Historical Society)

Below and middle: U.S. Custom House (1899–1907), New York, one of the
city's grandest Beaux-Arts buildings, with an elliptical domed rotunda.
(Irving Underhill, Museum of the City of New York; Nathaniel Lieberman)

St. Louis Art Museum (1904), a
formal composition. Its barrel-
vaulted roof is interrupted by
lunettes. (St. Louis Art Museum)

Opposite: U.S. Supreme Court
Building (1928–35), Washington,
D.C., a white marble temple of law.
(U.S. Supreme Court)

Woolworth Building (1910–13), New York, a 60-story building known as the Cathedral of Commerce. The ornamentation was inspired by French and English architecture. (Irving Underhill, Museum of the City of New York)

CRAM AND GOODHUE
Richard Oliver

Bertram Grosvenor Goodhue (1869–1924) was born in the ancestral home of the Grosvenors in Pomfret, Conn. He received little formal education and at age 15 began an apprenticeship in the architectural office of Renwick, Aspinwall and Russell, still run by James Renwick, where he became renowned as an accomplished delineator. Throughout Goodhue's career, architecture schools in America stressed the methods of the Ecole des Beaux-Arts in Paris, encouraging the almost exclusive use of the classical language of architecture, but Goodhue regarded classicism as rule-bound, academic and dry.

In 1891 Goodhue won a competition for the Cathedral of St. Matthew to be built in Dallas. Goodhue approached Ralph Adams Cram and Charles Francis Wentworth of Boston about associating with them to carry out the commission. As a result, the firm of Cram, Wentworth and Goodhue was established in 1892. In 1897 Charles Wentworth died, and the firm name was changed to Cram, Goodhue and Ferguson in 1898.

Ralph Adams Cram (1863–1942) was born in Hampton Falls, N.H. After first considering a career as an artist, he turned to architecture and from 1881 to 1886 worked for the firm of Rotch and Tilden. During a trip to Europe in 1887, he attended Christmas Eve mass in Rome and was struck by a vision of Roman Catholic tradition with its social, cultural and architectural implications.

Like Augustus Charles Pugin and subsequent Gothic Revival architects, Cram and Goodhue aspired to design buildings that began with an articulate and functional plan yielding vigorously composed, artistic masses enriched with expressive symbolism and built with a craftsman's attitude toward construction. They did not restrict themselves to the Gothic, however. Their 1893 competitive design for a proposed city hall for New York was classical, and they also designed a series of libraries in varied styles. The collaboration between Cram and Goodhue was a complex matter. Cram wrote and lectured extensively in an attempt to carry his ideas to a larger public, while Goodhue preferred to let his ideas emerge within his drawings and in the buildings themselves.

Winning the competition for the additions (1903–10) to the U.S. Military Academy at West Point, N.Y., secured the firm's national reputation. At this time a New York office, headed by Goodhue, was opened, and the two offices operated with increasing artistic independence. St. Thomas's Church (1906–13), New York, the last collaborative effort between Goodhue and Cram, is a distinguished Gothic Revival work featuring innovative vaulting techniques and contemporary iconography. The firm was dissolved in 1913, and Goodhue set up his own practice in New York.

Cram continued to practice with Ferguson, his vision of the Gothic culminating in his design for the Cathedral of St. John the Divine (1915–41), New York. A prolific author, he also served as professor of architectural philosphy and head of the architecture school at the Massachusetts Institute of Technology.

Goodhue's designs reflect his attempts to move away from conventional styles and uses of ornament. His

Elevation drawing and chantry of St. Thomas's Church (1905–13), New York. (St. Thomas's Church Archives; Museum of the City of New York)

Ralph Adams Cram, c. 1927. (MIT Museum)

Bertram Goodhue. (Ticor Collection, San Diego Historical Society)

theatrical buildings for the Panama-California Exposition (1911–15), San Diego, gave impetus to the Spanish colonial revival. In his design for the new St. Bartholomew's Church (1914–18), New York, Goodhue moved away from Gothic to a Romanesque-Byzantine idiom. The National Academy of Sciences Building (1919–24), Washington, D.C., featured freshly conceived stripped classical forms on the exterior balanced by a richly tiled central rotunda. His striking and enigmatic design for the Nebraska State Capitol (1920–32), Lincoln, fused elements of many styles into one vigorous composition culminating in a central tower that embodied the romantic image of a skyscraper.

Goodhue's fundamental artistic goal remained constant throughout his career: He always attempted to reconceive traditional forms in a personal and imaginative way, free of the rules of orthodox styles, and his fresh traditionalism presaged modern architecture. In 1925 the American Institute of Architects honored him with its Gold Medal. ◣

Cadet Chapel (1903–10), U.S. Military Academy, West Point, N.Y., reflecting a bold scale, rugged Gothic forms and dramatic composition. (U.S. Military Academy Archives)

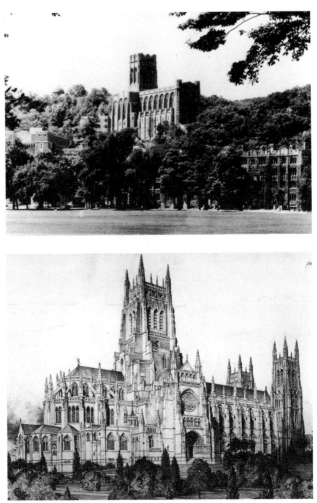

Cathedral of St. John the Divine (1915–41), New York, a landmark of the American Gothic Revival. (Cram and Ferguson)

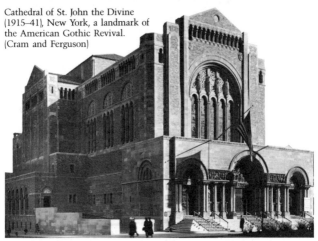

St. Bartholomew's Church (1914–19), New York, designed in a Roman-esque-Byzantine idiom, reflecting Goodhue's bolder scale of planning and massing and wider palette of materials. (Irving Underhill, Museum of the City of New York)

Panama-California Exposition (1911–15), San Diego, planned by Goodhue, who rejected City Beautiful principles in favor of a scheme to evoke the plan and spirit of an idealized Spanish city. (SDHS)

Perspective of the proposed campus (1917), California Institute of Technology, Pasadena, inspired by Spanish and Latin American universities. (CIT Archives)

Elevation submitted for the design competition for the Nebraska State Capitol (1920–32). The horizontal base serves as a foil for the soaring tower, which terminates in a tiled dome and Lee Lawrie's statue of a sower. (Nebraska State Historical Society)

Frederick C. Robie House (1909), Chicago, whose overlapping and sliding planes and blocklike piers show how close Wright's architecture was to cubism at this time. (Cervin Robinson, HABS)

William H. Winslow House (1893), River Forest, Ill., showing monumentality, symmetry and a strong sense of repose. (HABS)

Frank Lloyd Wright, c. 1936. (Bill Hedrich, Hedrich-Blessing)

Ward Willits House (1901), Highland Park, Ill., the prototypal Prairie house. (Ernst Wasmuth, *Drawings and Plans of Frank Lloyd Wright*)

FRANK LLOYD WRIGHT
H. Allen Brooks

The architecture of Frank Lloyd Wright (1867–1959) is marked by a richness of conception, unity of expression and fertility of invention that unerringly honor the fundamental laws of design while drawing strength and inspiration from a profound respect for American traditions, landscapes and native materials. Moreover, his designs destroyed once and for all our age-old idea of interior space—that a room was the space enclosed by four walls—by creating interiors that were defined rather than strictly enclosed. By this means the measurable values that had previously characterized interior space gave way to a space whose perimeters were no longer absolute but gauged by the ever-changing position of the beholder. As a consequence, the space seems, psychologically, much larger, more restful and more varied than its actual dimensions would suggest, with the result that a comparatively small house or office not only appears much bigger than it is but also serves a greater number of functions. For these reasons, architecture since Wright has been different from before, a fact that secures his position as America's greatest designer and one of the leading architects of all time.

Wright was born in Richland Center, Wis., and while working summers on his uncle's farm he acquired his deep respect for nature, natural materials and the agrarian way of life. He never attended architecture school, learning instead by apprenticeship, first with J. L. Silsbee and then for nearly six years with Louis Sullivan before entering private practice in 1893. His subsequent career, primarily devoted to residential architecture, divides into three periods of approximately 25 years each.

The first period, reaching maturity in 1900 and continuing until World War I, was characterized by the so-called prairie house. These long, low buildings, with broadly overhanging low-pitched roofs and often without an attic or basement, integrated comfortably into the flat prairie landscape, their rows of casement windows and extended wall surfaces emphasizing the horizontal dimension and thus helping create a powerful and restful sense of repose. Materials were of the region, the woodwork being neither planed nor painted, only stained against the weather. These were the years of many important residences—the Ward Willits House (1901), Highland Park, Ill.; the Darwin D. Martin House (1904), Buffalo; the Edwin H. Cheney House (1904), Oak Park, Ill.; the

Unity Temple (1906), Oak Park, Ill. The most abstract of Wright's early designs, these blocklike forms are thought to have been inspired by Froebel kindergarten toys. (© Frank Lloyd Wright Foundation)

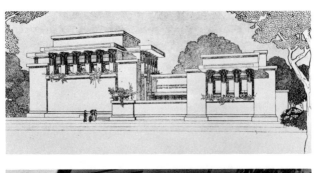

Living and dining rooms, Taliesin (1911), Spring Green, Wis. The exposed stone walls were built with materials from the site, and the furniture was designed by Wright. (© Frank Lloyd Wright Foundation)

Wright with his students in the atelier at Taliesin. (Hedrich-Blessing)

Frederick C. Robie House (1909), Chicago; and the Avery Coonley House (1908), Riverside, Ill.—a design progression that moved increasingly toward greater abstraction. Near the end of this period Wright built his own home, Taliesin, at Spring Green, Wis. In nondomestic architecture he strove for greater monumentality while inventing powerful yet beautifully integrated forms that expressed the diverse functional parts of the building, the Larkin Administration Building (1904), Buffalo, and Unity Temple (1906), Oak Park, Ill., being widely known.

Wright did not work in isolation but, along with Sullivan, was at the head of a vital and highly creative movement known as the Prairie School. These were the years of the Arts and Crafts movement and Craftsman and Mission furniture, as well as the California bungalow, all of which were interrelated with the Prairie School and, like it, succumbed to the new wave of conservatism and revivalism that followed World War I.

During Wright's second period, which lasted until the mid-1930s, he executed few commissions apart from the Imperial Hotel (1913–22), Tokyo, which he had designed before the war. These years, however, proved immensely inventive as he experimented and developed a whole new grammar of architectural forms and structures based on geometric shapes other than the square and rectangle— acute and obtuse angles, octagons, hexagons, circles and arcs. This experimentation provided him and countless others with an entirely new vocabulary that he exploited during the final quarter century before his death in 1959, the spiral Guggenheim Museum (1943–59), New York, being the best known.

The 1920s and early 1930s saw him turn increasingly to the written word, and in 1932, at the age of 65, he published *An Autobiography*, which, along with his other articles, books and lectures, introduced a new, nationwide audience to his ideas and brought him an increasing number of clients and commissions. That same year he founded the Taliesin Fellowship for training young architects.

Wright's third great period began in 1936 with three stunningly different designs—Fallingwater (1936), Bear Run, Pa.; the Johnson Wax Administration Building and Research Tower (1936, 1944), Racine, Wis.; and the Paul R. Hanna House (1936), Stanford, Calif. He also returned to the problem of the small, single-family house, and, while incorporating all of the spatial ideas originally invented for the prairie house, he produced a much more modest type known as the Usonian house, a name derived from "United States of North America." Of these he built dozens of variations beginning in 1937, the year he began a new desert home and studio near Phoenix, the second Taliesin, now extensively remodeled. In all he built some 400 buildings, having designed at least twice that many during a working career of 72 years. In 1949 he was awarded the American Institute of Architects' Gold Medal for his architectural achievements. ◩

Opposite: Mrs. George M. Millard House (1923), Pasadena, Calif., one of a series of concrete textile-block houses built by Wright in California in the 1920s. (Wayne Andrews, Archives of American Art)

Price Tower (1952), Bartlesville, Okla., embodying a new system of construction based on the form of a tree, in which a central shaft of reinforced concrete supports the cantilevered floor slabs. (Wm. Edmund Barrett)

Plan of Paul R. Hanna House (1936), Stanford, Calif., built on a hexagonal module. (Museum of Modern Art)

Pope-Leighey House (1940–41), Mount Vernon, Va., a Usonian house. (Jack E. Boucher, HABS)

Opposite: Fallingwater (1936), Bear Run, Pa. (John A. Burns, AIA)

Section of the Guggenheim Museum (1943–59), New York. (© Frank Lloyd Wright Foundation)

Studio of Frank Lloyd Wright (1898–1909), Oak Park, Ill., where Wright trained many young architects and draftsmen. (Ernst Wasmuth, *Drawings and Plans of Frank Lloyd Wright*)

Marin County Civic Center (1959–69), San Raphael, Calif. The dome and arch forms characterized Wright's later work. (© Ezra Stoller, ESTO)

GREENE AND GREENE
Randell L. Makinson

The Arts and Crafts movement achieved its greatest
fulfillment in America in the works of the architects
Greene and Greene during the first two decades of the
20th century. Most noted for their carefully articulated
wood residences, the Greenes' influence was widespread
and their names often identified with the California
bungalow. The Greenes not only charted new courses in
American architecture and related interiors and furnishings but also established higher standards of construction.

Charles Sumner Greene (1868–1957) and Henry Mather
Greene (1870–1954) were born near Cincinnati but spent
much of their formative years on their grandparents' farm
in West Virginia. The brothers were nearing high school
age when their father set up medical practice in St. Louis,
where they were soon enrolled in Calvin Woodward's
experimental manual training program sponsored by
Washington University. Through this program they gained
invaluable insight into the characteristics and techniques
of wood, metals, tools and machinery, as well as an
understanding of the craft of construction methods.
Steeped in the logic of function, materials and form, the
brothers were not sympathetic to the Beaux-Arts architectural training they received during their two years of
study at the Massachusetts Institute of Technology,
although they were enriched by their studies of scale,
proportion and optics.

After almost a decade of practice in Pasadena, Calif., in
1902 they burst forth seemingly overnight with their own
architectural language in their designs for their own
homes (1902 and 1904), the James Culbertson House
(1902), with furnishings by Gustav Stickley, and the
Arturo Bandini House (1903), with its open courtyard
plan, all in Pasadena. By 1904 elements of their new
expression came together for the first time in the Jennie
A. Reeves House (1904) and the Adelaide Tichenor House
(1904), both in Long Beach. By 1907 their work was fully
refined as demonstrated in the Pasadena houses for
Freeman A. Ford (1907), Robert R. Blacker (1907), David B.
Gamble (1908), Charles M. Pratt (1909) and William R.
Thorsen (1909) and the Crow-Crocker House (1909). By
1911 the Greenes were using gunite, which allowed for
softer forms, in the designs of the estates for Cordelia
Culbertson (1911), Pasadena, and Mortimer Fleishhacker
(1911), Woodside, Calif. Following his semiretirement to
Carmel in 1918, Charles independently began construction of the D. L. James House, Carmel, his noted stone
masterwork, and in 1928 Henry Greene designed the last
house by either brother—the Walter L. Richardson Ranch
House, Porterville, one of his most powerful compositions.

During their close working relationship with the wood
craftsmen Peter and John Hall and glass artisan Emile
Lange, the Greenes' most sophisticated designs came to
fruition. Between 1905 and 1911 their more affluent
clientele enabled them to exercise their talents to the
fullest, encompassing gardens and landscapes and completely integrated interiors, including furniture, carpets,
lighting fixtures, stained glass and fabrics. Work diminished in the following decade because of the high costs of

Charles Sumner Greene, c. 1906. (Los Angeles Public Library)

Henry Mather Greene, c. 1906. (Los Angeles Public Library)

Charles J. Willett House (1905), Pasadena, Calif. Its modest but tasteful scale set the pattern for bungalow home designs used by builders and architects throughout the country. (*The Western Architect*, 1908)

James W. Neill House (1906), Pasadena, Calif., featuring exposed timbers, a massive boulder and clinker brick wall, natural shingle siding and a pergola across the brick-paved drive. (Marvin Rand)

Highback living room chair designed for the David B. Gamble House. Gustav Stickley's designs for furniture encouraged the Greenes to create their own. (Marvin Rand)

David B. Gamble House (1908), Pasadena, Calif. The cantilevers, roof lines, sleeping porches, terraces and wide stairways create a dynamic horizontal effect. (Marvin Rand)

Entry hall, Robert R. Blacker House (1907), Pasadena, Calif., featuring stained-glass doors and lamps and paneling in teak and mahogany. (Whitland Locke)

D. L. James House (1918), Carmel, Calif., a stone structure that seems to have grown out of the rocky cliffs. (L. S. Slevin)

Plan of Charles M. Pratt House
(1909), designed in a relaxed U-
form. (Greene and Greene Library,
David B. Gamble House)

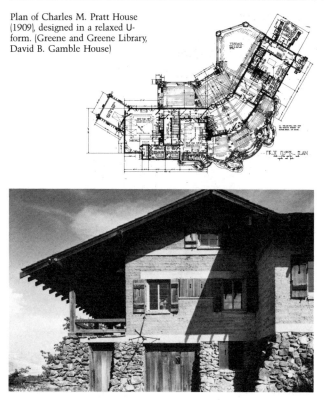

Walter L. Richardson Ranch House (1928), Porterville, Calif., built of adobe
from the site and detailed for construction by the ranch hands. (Marvin Rand)

their construction and less venturesome clients.

The magic in the work of the Greene brothers was
sparked by their richly different personalities. Henry often
referred to Charles as the "artist" whose deep devotion to
his architecture left him sometimes oblivious to everyday
happenings around him. Complementing Charles's ram-
pant and creative imagination, Henry Greene's disciplined
personality, interest in engineering and devotion to system
and order brought to the work, the office and the craft a
careful and sophisticated restraint.

Following World War II their work received steadily
growing acclaim, and in 1952 they were hailed by the
American Institute of Architects in a special citation as
"formulators of a new and native architecture . . .
recognized throughout the world, influencing the design
of small as well as great houses." 🔲

BERNARD MAYBECK
Richard Longstreth

Bernard Maybeck (1862–1957) considered every constraint in architecture to be an opportunity. No budget was too small, no site too constrained, no client too demanding. He relished the process of design and of supervising construction. For Maybeck, creating architecture was an intensely personal endeavor, yet, in the final analysis, a building's value was measured by its conduciveness to the activities of others. For reasons such as these, he does not seem to have minded that the material success sought by many colleagues always eluded him.

Raised in New York amid a community of German-American intellectuals and craftsmen, Maybeck studied at the Ecole des Beaux-Arts in Paris from 1882 to 1886. On returning to the United States, he entered the office of Carrère and Hastings, which was then rapidly gaining widespread acclaim. Yet, the promise of the future dimmed when Maybeck set out on his own in 1889. Moving first to Kansas City and then to San Francisco, he held a succession of jobs, few of them consequential. Maybeck did not see a design realized until 1895 and did not open an office until 1902. Over the next 36 years he enjoyed a steady, if modest, flow of commissions. Most projects were for inexpensive suburban houses. He coveted designing grand civic and institutional complexes, but the majority of these projects remained on paper. Maybeck had a devoted band of admirers among Berkeley residents and earned the respect of some Bay Area colleagues. For most of his life, however, he was considered an eccentric in appearance, demeanor and practice—an engaging architect but hardly an important one. In an era when conventions were venerated, he epitomized the unconventional.

Maybeck's work is unusually diverse in its use of form, space, scale, materials and expression. With equal facility he could design a small rustic cottage such as the Boke House (1901–02), Berkeley, or an elaborate classical public building such as the Palace of Fine Arts (1913–15), San Francisco; employ vernacular or high-style imagery; or use structure to create rich visual effects or cover it with theatrical surface embellishments. In some cases, a strong sense of order and unity pervade a scheme; in others, the

Men's Dormitory, Principia College (1930–38), Elsah, Ill. Maybeck's last major commission, designed in association with Julia Morgan, was a fanciful interpretation of a postmedieval English village, offering a rural counterpoint to Collegiate Gothic campus designs. (Principia College)

Bernard Maybeck, c. 1910. (Documents Collection, College of Environmental Design, University of California, Berkeley)

Leon L. Roos House (1908–09), San Francisco, larger than most of Maybeck's houses but characteristic in its complex massing and intricate details. (Documents Collection, CED, University of California, Berkeley)

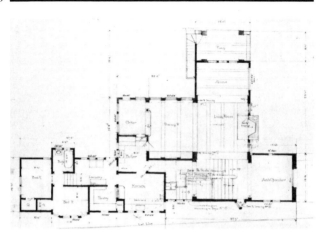

Plan for the J. H. Senger House (1906–07), Berkeley, Calif. The inventiveness of Maybeck's spatial sequences can be seen in the constantly turning stair hall. (Documents Collection, CED, University of California, Berkeley)

Right and below: First Church of Christ, Scientist (1909–11), Berkeley, Calif., Maybeck's most famous work. The sanctuary interior was made spatially complex by large concrete piers and a web of wooden trusses. (Documents Collection, CED, University of California, Berkeley; Roy Flamm)

Andrew Lawson House (1907–08), Berkeley, Calif. Built of reinforced concrete, it is one of Maybeck's most elemental designs. (Richard Longstreth)

Palace of Fine Arts (1913–15), San Francisco. Constructed for the Panama-Pacific International Exposition, this is the only one of Maybeck's numerous grand classical schemes to be realized. (Library of the California Historical Society)

appearance is so casual as to suggest that no designer was involved. Space could be linear and processional or circuitous and rambling. Maybeck could impart a greater feeling of fantasy than any other architect of his generation, but he could also give his buildings a clear, purposeful character.

Maybeck was not a theoretician, yet he was deeply influenced by ideas as dissimilar as those held by the French academic tradition and the Arts and Crafts movement. He believed that architecture should express ties to past cultures. At the same time, he was continually experimenting. Standard arrangements of form and space were avoided as if no precedent for a given problem existed. This unceasing appetite for invention sometimes led to fragmentary results; nevertheless, his work is almost always interesting and often memorable. And however unorthodox, Maybeck's designs possess sensitivity to site, climate and use. The needs of the client were never subordinated to concerns for art or ideology.

Although admired by modern architects in the Bay Area from the 1930s, Maybeck did not receive national recognition until after World War II. In 1951 the American Institute of Architects honored him with its Gold Medal. The individuality of his work has discouraged imitations; however, the inventiveness and freedom of expression these buildings manifest have in various ways inspired several generations of practitioners.

JULIA MORGAN
Sara Holmes Boutelle

Julia Morgan (1872–1957), a San Francisco native who practiced as head of her own office for 46 years, evokes a quality of mystery even when the facts of her life are known. She was a five-foot-tall, Berkeley-trained engineer, the first woman in the world to be accepted in architecture at the Ecole des Beaux-Arts, and she designed nearly 800 buildings, including the spectacular Hearst Castle at San Simeon. Yet, Morgan sought anonymity, avoiding publicity as if it violated the spirit of her craft.

After a six-year stint in Paris, Morgan returned to a job at the University of California at Berkeley under the architect John Galen Howard, who boasted of "the best and most talented designer whom I have to pay almost nothing, as it is a woman." She worked at the university for two years, notably as project designer for the reinforced concrete Greek Theater (1902–04), but this project only whetted her appetite for independent private practice. Morgan established her own office in San Francisco in 1904. Her profession was her life, chosen as a vocation and pursued with undeviating energy. She dealt alone with clients as diverse as William Randolph Hearst and a local high school mathematics teacher, counting most of them as her friends and many as repeat clients. Morgan hired engineers, designers and office staff to carry out the many projects, but she herself was on the site checking contractors, crafts workers and materials with meticulous attention to detail. Her office became like a family, carried through illnesses and the depression, sharing in profits at the end of each year.

Most conspicuous of Morgan's large-scale works is San Simeon (1919–39), designed for Hearst on a hilltop overlooking the Pacific along California's central coast. For 20 years she traveled there almost every weekend to supervise construction, consulting with the client by correspondence during the week from her city office. Other large works include early campus buildings at Mills College (1904–16), Oakland; the Asilomar Conference Center (1913–29), near Monterey; and group housing and

Julia Morgan, in 1898 as a student in Paris and in 1927. (Both, Special Collections, California Polytechnic State University)

Interior (1907), First Baptist Church, Oakland, Calif., redesigned by Morgan after its collapse in the 1906 earthquake. The curve of the pews balances the octagonal ceiling supports. (James H. Edelen)

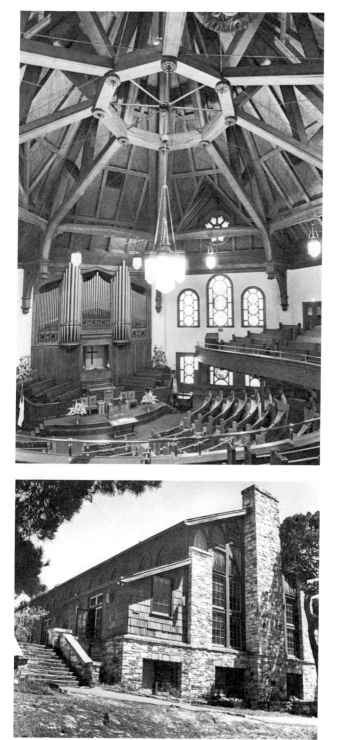

Merrill Hall (1928), Asilomar Conference Center, near Monterey, Calif., sited on a slope to maintain a horizontal feeling while allowing a powerful vertical statement at the end of the building. (James H. Edelen)

La Casa Grande at San Simeon (1919–39), the main house of Hearst's luxurious California complex, combining elements of Mediterranean architecture. (California Division of Beaches and Parks)

The Neptune Pool at San Simeon, with the portico of a Roman temple. (California Department of Natural Resources)

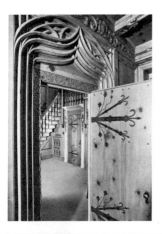

Interior, Bear House (1930), Wyntoon, Calif. The door to the living room has detailed carving and intricate ironwork characteristic of Morgan's attention to craftsmanship. (James H. Edelen)

Turner Stores (1942), Berkeley, Calif. This shopping center, whose arch was originally open, shows Morgan's artful placement of the shop entrances so they do not open directly onto the street. (James H. Edelen)

recreation facilities for the YWCA in San Jose, Oakland, Long Beach, Fresno, Pasadena, Hollywood, Salt Lake City and Honolulu. In this period Morgan also developed the Wyntoon estate (1931–42) for Hearst in northern California. Meanwhile, she designed churches, schools, women's clubs, a hotel, hospitals, commercial buildings, many swimming pools and hundreds of residences. There was literally no time or space for a private life.

Morgan's training at the Ecole and her deep love of her native state's landscape and history formed the greatest influence on her design. The site and the program indicated by the client were more significant than any influence of specific architects. Bernard Maybeck was her teacher, first employer, lifelong friend (they both died in 1957, he at 95, she at 85) and sometime collaborator. Their work together includes the Lawson House (1895), Berkeley, the Phoebe Hearst Memorial Gymnasium (1926), Berkeley, campus buildings for Principia College (1930s), Elsah, Ill., and a projected columbarium south of San Francisco in the mid-1940s. Their collaboration was harmonious, but their differences were greater than their similarities.

Morgan's legacy seems to be more philosophical than graphic: a sense of high standards in work, a joy in the California landscape and an empathic quality that made her remarkably able to realize her clients' wishes, which contributed to her almost incredible achievements. ◹

ADDISON MIZNER
Donald W. Curl

Addison Cairns Mizner (1872–1933), the son of a
prominent pioneer family of California, was apprenticed
in the San Francisco office of Willis Polk and traveled
extensively in the Pacific, Central America and Europe
before deciding in 1904 to become a New York society
architect in the mold of his idol, Stanford White. Through
Mrs. Herman Oelrichs, the former Tessie Fair of San
Francisco and a grande dame of New York society, Mizner
met White, the designer of her white marble palace in
Newport. Mizner later said that his first New York work
came from commissions "too small" for the McKim,
Mead and White office.

Although Mizner's reputation as a society architect
came from his flamboyant Palm Beach villas built in the
1920s in the Spanish and Italian revival styles, he laid the
framework for his Florida success in the period between
1904 and 1917, when he completed numerous northern
projects. Even in these years he designed several Spanish-
style houses. One of these, a house for William Prime
(1911), Brookville, N.Y., became, after many additions,
Hillwood, the Tudor-style mansion of Marjorie Mer-
riweather Post.

When the United States's entry into World War I
brought a halt to residential construction, Mizner accepted the invitation of Paris Singer, the sewing machine heir,
to visit Palm Beach. Shortly after Mizner's arrival in
January 1918, Singer commissioned him to design a
convalescent hospital for shell-shocked soldiers that could
later serve as a private social club. Mizner commented
that the site on the shores of Lake Worth suggested a
Spanish building with Venetian and Spanish colonial
elements. The war ended before construction was completed, so the building was never used as a hospital. It
opened in January 1919 as the Everglades Club and
immediately became the exclusive new center of Palm
Beach resort life.

As an attractive and romantic alternative to the
existing frame and shingle, northeastern seashore–style
buildings of the resort, the club's architectural success
soon equalled its social triumph. Before the season's end
the fashionableness of the style was confirmed when
Mizner received the commission for a great oceanfront
villa from Mrs. Edward T. Stotesbury, wife of the
Philadelphia banker and undisputed leader of Palm Beach
society.

Mizner's architectural style swept the resort; almost all
construction for the next six years, no matter who the
architect, was in a Mediterranean revival style. The period
1920–26 was also Mizner's most productive. In 1923 alone
he designed Playa Riente, his most magnificent Palm
Beach mansion, for Joshua Cosden, an Oklahoma oil
millionaire; 11 other large villas for society clients such
as Anthony J. Drexel Biddle, Angier Biddle Duke and
Rodman Wanamaker II; a clubhouse for the Gulfstream
Golf Club; and a studio and office building for himself,
which became the first section of the Via Mizner complex
of stores, apartments, offices and restaurants. He also
remodeled the houses of Henry C. Phipps and J. Leonard
Replogle. To supply "authentic" materials he also

Addison Mizner. (Historical Society of Palm Beach County)

Everglades Club (1918–19), Palm Beach, Fla. It had a great dining room seating 200 on the first floor and apartments for Singer and Mizner in the tower. (© Craig Kuhner)

established Mizner Industries, which produced handmade barrel tiles and pottery, cast-stone door and window surrounds, decorative wrought-iron work and lighting fixtures and even the furniture used to decorate his houses.

In 1925, at the height of the Florida land boom, Mizner became a land developer, promoting the new resort of Boca Raton. Unfortunately, the boom peaked just as he inaugurated his project. Although Boca Raton real estate sold well for six months, by the late fall of 1925 the boom was over. The collapse led to the loss of Mizner's own fortune and health, the bankruptcy of his development and the decline in fashion for his architecture. Although he continued his Palm Beach practice until his death in 1933, he never attained his earlier success. Nonetheless, during his decade and a half in Palm Beach, Mizner's Spanish revival buildings revolutionized architectural design in the town and set an identifying style for the state in the 1920s. ⌖

William Gray Warden House (1922), Palm Beach, Fla. A loggia affording views of ocean and patio became a trademark of Mizner's design. (© Craig Kuhner)

Joshua Cosden House (Playa Riente) (1923), Palm Beach, Fla., Mizner's largest house. The great hall, made of stone, had a rib-vaulted ceiling supported by twisted columns to emphasize height and space; a double staircase rose to the main level of the house. (Steven Seiden)

Opposite: George S. Rasmussen House (Casa Nana) (1926), Palm Beach, Fla., whose windows show Mizner's fondness for Venetian Gothic motifs. (© Craig Kuhner)

Via Mizner (1923–24), Palm Beach,
Fla., which became one of the most
fashionable shopping thoroughfares
in the world. (© Craig Kuhner)

Gulfstream Golf Club (1923), Palm
Beach, Fla., a small structure given
added importance by the arcaded
loggia and double flight of curving
stairs. (© Craig Kuhner)

IRVING J. GILL
David Gebhard and Bruce Kamerling

Since 1910 Irving J. Gill (1870–1936) has been seen as an avant-garde innovator. Early on he was described as a "secessionist," and his architecture was equated with cubism because of his use of concrete and the concrete tilt-slab system of construction and his elimination of the traditional array of interior and exterior moldings and details. Gill was rediscovered in the 1920s and, in the late 1950s, was enshrined as a pioneer of the International Style through the writings of Esther McCoy.

Gill was born on his father's farm near Tully, N.Y. At the age of 19 he went to nearby Syracuse and entered the architectural office of Ellis G. Hall. After one year he joined Joseph L. Silsbee in Chicago and then in 1891 Adler and Sullivan. After two years in this office he moved to San Diego, where he worked independently and with various partners until after 1910, when he moved his office to Los Angeles. In the late 1920s he returned to the San Diego area and remained there until his death.

Gill's first designs in San Diego reflect the full range of styles then being built, from the English Tudor and the American colonial revival to the classicism of the Beaux-Arts. He and his partners were caught up as well in the then-emerging Mission Revival and the accompanying Craftsman movement. In much of his work before 1907, it is difficult to separate Gill's approach from those of his partners. But even in these early years there are hints of his interest in simple, pristine surfaces and volumes—in his Shingle Style Granger Music Hall (1896), National City, Calif., where a pair of oversized circular windows dominates the principal facade, and in his Waldo Waterman House (1900), San Diego, a sculptural granite Craftsman cottage.

In 1907 Gill produced his first cubist stucco box, the Allen House in Bonita, Calif. This abstraction of the Mission Revival reflects not only his own predilections but probably also those of his associate Frank Meade, who was fascinated with the primitive qualities of North African architecture. From this point on Gill concentrated on the synthesis of the mission and Native American

Irving J. Gill, c. 1910. (San Diego Historical Society)

Opposite: Granger Music Hall (1896), National City, Calif., housing an accoustically perfect recital hall. (Ticor Collection, SDHS)

Waldo Waterman House (1900), San Diego, an English-style design typical of William Hebbard and Gill's work at the turn of the century. (Ticor Collection, SDHS)

Bentham Hall and Tower (1909), Bishop's School, La Jolla, Calif. The buildings of the complex are tied to the site by their long arcades. (Ticor Collection, SDHS)

La Jolla Women's Club (1912–14), La Jolla, Calif., built using the tilt-slab technique. The repeated arches and trellised pergolas subtly suggest the influence of California's mission architecture. (Marvin Rand, HABS)

Allen House (1907), Bonita, Calif., Gill's first essay into totally stripped-down architecture. Nature provides the only ornament—the vine on the trellis. (Ticor Collection, SDHS)

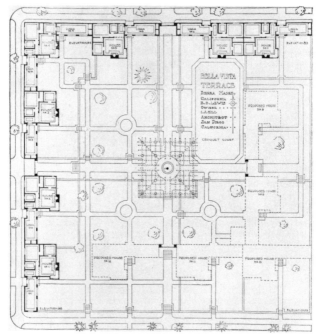

Bella Vista Terrace (1910), Sierra Madre, Calif., one of Gill's first major designs for low-income housing. (SDHS)

Opposite: South Bay Union Elementary School (1929), San Diego, Gill's personal adaptation of the Art Deco Style. (Ticor Collection, SDHS)

pueblo images by reducing them to their basic forms: the cube, the circle, the rectangle and the line. His designs often consisted of a rectangular cube, articulated by a pattern of rectangular openings and held to its site by a projecting loggia defined by a row of arched openings. This approach can be seen in his buildings at the Bishop School (1909, 1916), the La Jolla Women's Club (1912–14) and his building for the Scripps Playground (1914), all in La Jolla. Even more abstracted from the mission and pueblo images were his Scripps House (1915–16), La Jolla, the Dodge House (1914–16), Hollywood, and the Horatio West Court (1919), Santa Monica.

Along with the Olmsted brothers and Lloyd Wright, Gill was involved in the planning of the new industrial town of Torrance (1911–15), designing the principal commercial buildings in the city center. Throughout his career Gill was intensely concerned with the design of houses for workers. As early as 1908 he had established a prototype in his small three-room cottages at the end of Robinson Mew, San Diego. He worked out variations of this theme in his bungalow court, Bella Vista Terrace (1913), Sierra Madre, and in his Workman's Cottages (1913), Torrance. Gill also participated in the early planning of the Panama-California Exposition (1911–15), San Diego, the final design for which was done by Bertram Goodhue.

In his later designs he continued his references to the mission and pueblo traditions, as in the city hall and the fire and police station (both 1929), Oceanside, Calif. In other projects he assimilated and enhanced the Art Deco style, as in his South Bay Union Elementary School (1929), San Diego, designed with John Siebert.

Gill's architecture not only provides a bridge to the International Style of the 1920s and later but also illustrates how a designer synthesizes and infuses new life into traditional architectural images. ◪

RICHARD NEUTRA
Alson Clark

The life of no other 20th-century architect so epitomized the term International Style as that of Richard Neutra (1892–1970). Practitioner, author and lecturer, he gained worldwide recognition as an advocate of modern design. In the United States, he had a strong influence on architecture, particularly in California. Born in Vienna, a center of the evolving new culture, Neutra attended the Technische Hochschule, where he was influenced by the work of Otto Wagner and also knew Adolf Loos, famous for his polemical equation of ornament with crime. Loos first interested Neutra in America, an interest that was whetted when Neutra discovered the first European publication of the work of Frank Lloyd Wright.

After service in World War I, Neutra worked in Germany, where, in 1921, he became a collaborator of the architect Erich Mendelsohn. In 1922 he married Dione Niedermann, and in 1923 the Neutras came to America, where he worked for Wright briefly at Taliesin and for Holabird and Roche in Chicago, an experience that formed the subject of his first book, *Wie Baut Amerika?*, published in Stuttgart in 1927.

In 1925 the Neutras arrived in Los Angeles, living with the architect R. M. Schindler, a friend from Vienna days, until 1930. The Lovell (Health) House (1929), Los Angeles, with balconies suspended by steel cables from the roof frame, was, in retrospect, one of the most important works of his career. The open-web skeleton was transported to the steep hillside by truck. When the house was featured in Neutra's second book, *Amerika,* published in Vienna in 1930, he was hailed as a technological wizard. He returned to Europe in 1930 and was asked to lecture at the Bauhaus and in Japan.

Neutra's architecture was usually rectangular and straight-lined, unmistakably man-made, yet always sensitive to the site. One of his books, for example, was entitled *Mysteries and Realities of the Site* (1951). The slender, repetitive steel skeletons of his work may show the influence of Japan, of the imaginative Schindler or of Wright, but the synthesis was always Neutra's.

Opposite and above: Lovell (Health) House (1929), Los Angeles, the first completely steel-framed residence in the United States. The living room, with furniture designed by Neutra, reveals exhilarating spaces. (Both, Luckhaus Studio, Special Collections, University Research Library, UCLA)

Richard Neutra. (Bettina, Special Collections, University Research Library, University of California, Los Angeles)

The years before World War II saw the completion of the Beard House (1934), Altadena, Calif., and the country house for Joseph von Sternberg (1935), San Fernando Valley, Calif., both constructed of the latest prefabricated steel sandwich panels. Scarcity of steel during the war forced Neutra to use wood in the elegant, open Nesbitt House (1943), Los Angeles. Because of its economy he employed wood in many of his postwar residential commissions, of which the Moore House (1952), Ojai, Calif., is a good example. The plane of the water of the pool, a natural element favored by Neutra in later years, echoes the planar quality of the architecture and is complemented by the lush landscaping, producing a lyrical synthesis of natural and built elements.

In the postwar years resistence to modern architecture evaporated, and the time seemed ripe for Neutra to cap his career with the major public commissions that had eluded him. To that end he formed a partnership with Robert Alexander, and an example of their work is the Los Angeles County Hall of Records (1962). In his later career Neutra became unsure of himself and difficult to work with, and his public buildings never gained the recognition that had been accorded to his earlier work. Neutra died at Wuppertal, Germany, in 1970, while photographing one of his houses. In 1977 the American Institute of Architects honored him with its Gold Medal. ◣

Landfair Apartments (1935–37), Los
Angeles, a block of densely packed
row houses with staggered set-
backs. (Luckhaus Studio, Special
Collections, University Research Library, UCLA)

Channel Heights (1942), San Pedro,
Calif., federal housing for shipyard
workers. The 222 residential structures provided housing for 600
families. (Special Collections, University Research Library, UCLA)

Kaufmann House (1946), Palm
Springs, Calif., designed as an obvi-
ously man-made pavilion for inhab-
iting the desert. The side elevation
presents a study of geometric
shapes. (Both, Julius Shulman, Special Collections, University Research Library, UCLA)

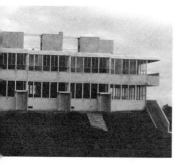

Moore House (1952), Ojai, Calif., an oasis in an arid valley. The pools served as reservoirs for irrigating the gardens and humidifying the air. (Julius Shulman, Special Collections, University Research Library, UCLA)

Garden Grove Community Church (1962, tower 1966), Garden Grove, Calif., a drive-in community church that preceded and still complements Philip Johnson's "Crystal Cathedral." (Garden Grove Community Church)

WALTER GROPIUS
James Marston Fitch

Although commonly thought of as an American, Walter Gropius (1883–1969) was actually a German who first came to the United States in 1937. Many of his most notable buildings, both here and overseas, were built after he became an American citizen, but the most famous of his projects—the Bauhaus, an institution that was to become synonymous with functional design—was created by him in the Weimar Republic. His fame on both sides of the Atlantic rested on two careers that developed in tandem—an academic career, in which he became one of the leading theoreticians of modern architecture, and a practicing career, in which he was a leading architect for a full half century before his death in 1969. In both areas, he played an internationally decisive role.

In Europe, even before World War I, Gropius achieved fame for such projects as his Pavilion for the Werkbund Exhibition at Cologne in 1914. In the following two decades, he designed a number of buildings, the most famous of which was the complex for the Bauhaus (1925) at Dessau, Germany. Largely on the basis of this school's astonishing prestige, he was invited to come to Harvard University to head the Graduate School of Design just before World War II.

Despite his long, prestigious career on both sides of the Atlantic, the number of constructed buildings that can be securely attributed to him is surprisingly limited. One reason is that many of his projects were never built—for example, the Total Theater for the great Berlin impresario Erwin Piscator. Another reason was that Gropius himself, although a supremely talented designer, always preferred

Below and opposite: Gropius House (1937, with Marcel Breuer), Lincoln, Mass., one of the first International Style houses in New England. The interior reflects the streamlined nature of the exterior. (Both, Damora, Society for the Preservation of New England Antiquities)

Bauhaus (1925), Dessau, Germany, for which Gropius designed the instruction building and the masters' houses. (Busch-Reisinger Museum, Harvard University)

Walter Gropius. (The Architects Collaborative)

New Kensington Housing Development (1941, with Marcel Breuer), New Kensington, Pa., a low-cost project for defense workers. (Gottscho-Schleisner, Busch-Reisinger Museum, Harvard University)

Harvard University Graduate Center (1949–50), Cambridge, Mass., a
functionalist structure that meets the needs of students' daily life and also
relates to the university's traditional environment. (TAC)

John F. Kennedy Federal Office Building (1966), Boston, built in an urban
setting designed by I. M. Pei. (© Ezra Stoller, ESTO)

Pan American Building (1963, with Pietro Belluschi), New York. By cutting the building's corners, Gropius created a prismatic effect that gives a sense of flow around and beyond the building. (Joseph Molitor, TAC)

teamwork. Thus, the firm that he established in Cambridge after his retirement from Harvard in 1952 was significantly named The Architects Collaborative (TAC); even here he preferred to be known merely as a member, one among equals. The American buildings in whose design he played a principal role are his own home (1937), Lincoln, Mass.; the Harvard University Graduate Center (1949–50), Cambridge, Mass.; the Pan American Building (1963), New York, which he designed with Pietro Belluschi; and the John F. Kennedy Federal Office Building (1966), Boston. Among TAC projects abroad in which Gropius played a key role are four in West Germany—the factories for the Rosenthal Ceramics Factory (1963), Selb, and the Thomas Glass Factory (1967), Amberg, as well as Gropiusstadt (1962), a large housing project in West Berlin—and the U.S. Embassy (1956), Athens, Greece, and the National University (1957), Baghdad, Iraq. The American Institute of Architects awarded its 1959 Gold Medal to Gropius and its 1964 Architectural Firm Award to The Architects Collaborative.

All of these projects are notable for their sobriety, rejection of historicizing ornament and disdain for the idiosyncratic formalism that characterized architecture at the end of the 19th century. Functionalist design, of which Gropius was at once a great pioneer and a great practitioner, had become the dominant idiom of world architecture by the time of his death. It had radically altered the appearance of every city on earth. But it had also become what Gropius himself had warned against—a style itself. As such, it was vulnerable to many of the charges that the Post-Modernists have hurled against it. However, it had permanently altered the direction of world architecture, and a new eclectic revival is not apt to alter this fact.

LUDWIG MIES VAN DER ROHE
David Spaeth

After Frank Lloyd Wright, Ludwig Mies van der Rohe (1886–1969) made the greatest contributions to 20th-century architecture. For Mies ("van der Rohe," a variation of his mother's name, was added after 1907), technology was the most significant force shaping this or any other time. His work celebrates this, raising the materials of the Industrial Revolution—glass, steel and reinforced concrete—to the realm of art.

Born to a modest stonecutter's family in Aachen, Germany, Mies had little opportunity for formal education. Until age 13 he attended Aachen's cathedral school and then trade school, followed by apprenticeship as a brick mason. Three years with a firm of interior decorators refined his freehand drawing talent; a short time in an architect's office developed his drafting skills.

Finding Aachen's opportunities limited, Mies moved to Berlin, where, after two years' further tutelage, he designed the Riehl House (1907), described as "a work so faultless" no one would guess it was the first independent work of a young architect. At age 23, feeling the need for further training, Mies entered the office of Europe's most influential architect, Peter Behrens, who employed two of modern architecture's future leaders, Walter Gropius and Charles-Edouard Jeanneret (Le Corbusier).

Experience in supervising war-related construction coupled with the artistic liberation occasioned by the kaiser's abdication unshackled Mies's creativity. During the early years of the Weimar Republic, Mies exhibited projects so visionary as to place him at the forefront of modern architecture. His furniture designs, successfully applying the cantilever principle, produced the most enduring symbol of excellence, the Barcelona chair (1929).

Between 1928 and 1930 he designed two important buildings, the German Pavilion and Industrial Exhibits at the International Exhibition, Barcelona, Spain, and the Tugendhat House, Brno, Czechoslovakia, both pure expressions of architectural space defined, not enclosed, by walls, floors and ceiling planes. In 1930 he was appointed director of the Bauhaus, and in 1931 his European career reached its zenith with his election to the Prussian Academy.

Hitler's assumption of power in 1933 made Mies's position untenable. During a 1937 visit to the United States, Mies was appointed director of architecture at Armour (later Illinois) Institute of Technology. In this

Top and above: Crown Hall (1950–56), Illinois Institute of Technology, Chicago, the first of Mies's large-scale "universal spaces," and preliminary perspective (1939) of his plan for IIT, a unified composition in which the buildings are related asymmetrically. (Both, Hedrich-Blessing)

Ludwig Mies van der Rohe. (Hedrich-Blessing)

position he founded a new department of architecture, produced a plan for the new campus and, until his retirement in 1958, designed all the campus buildings. Along Chicago's Lake Shore Drive he built the world's first all-glass apartment buildings (1948–51), and in Plano, Ill., the first all-glass residence, the Farnsworth House (1945–50). He designed the Seagram Building (1954–58, with Philip Johnson), New York's most elegant and, at the time, most expensive office building. As part of Detroit's renewal, Mies's Lafayette Park (1955–63) demonstrated that urban life could combine the best of city and country living. Like all his work, his last, Berlin's New National Gallery (1962–68), clarified the essential relationship between material and structure, between technology and the times.

Before his death he received for his contributions to architecture and education the 1959 Royal Gold Medal of the Royal Institute of British Architects, the 1960 Gold Medal of the American Institute of Architects, Germany's Order of Merit and the Presidential Medal of Freedom. ◿

Below and middle: 860–880
Lake Shore Drive Apartments
(1948–51), Chicago, whose
skin was constructed
solely of steel and
glass. Mies's Barcelona
chairs enhance the
lobby. (Both, Hedrich-
Blessing)

Farnsworth House (1945–50), Plano, Ill., which radically changed domestic
architecture. The sense of architectural space is heightened by the
cantilevered roof and floor planes. (Bill Hedrich, Hedrich-Blessing)

Seagram Building (1954–58, with Philip Johnson), New York, whose rich materials and unprecedented open space endow it with a monumental quality. (Courtesy Philip Johnson)

Cullinan Hall (1954–58), Houston Museum of Fine Arts. The exposed steel structure of the plate girders is the same as used in Crown Hall, but here the facade is curved. (Hedrich-Blessing)

Lafayette Park (1955–63), Detroit, an urban redevelopment scheme combining high-rise apartments and residential structures linked by open spaces restricted to pedestrians. (Hedrich-Blessing)

EERO SAARINEN
Peter C. Papademetriou

Eero Saarinen (1910–61) shared both the same birthdate and career with his father, Eliel, and the story of his career is nearly inseparable from that of his father until the elder Saarinen's death in 1950. In his mature design work, however, Eero Saarinen came into his own as an architect whose interests span a broad range of issues and capture the spirit of America in the decade 1950–60.

Eero was born in Finland and raised at Eliel's lakeside compound near Helsinki. Having received international recognition for his second-prize entry in the 1922 Chicago Tribune Building competition, Eliel relocated the family to Evanston, Ill., and then Ann Arbor, Mich. In 1925 the Saarinens moved to Birmingham, Mich., near Detroit, to oversee development of Cranbrook, a group of educational and artistic institutions created by publisher George Booth and designed by Eliel. In 1931 Eero entered Yale University to study architecture and was graduated with honors in 1934. He then traveled extensively in Europe, where he came in direct contact with the Scandinavian branch of the International Style.

On his return in 1936, Eero entered into practice with Eliel, asserting his own interests in technology and contemporary issues. In 1938 he went to the office of Norman Bel Geddes in New York and was designer for the General Motors Futurama pavilion of the 1939 New York World's Fair. During this period, the Saarinens began to receive national attention as proponents of the new evolving modern style through several completed buildings and competitions. With the advent of World War II, the firm became Saarinen and Swanson, designing a number of Department of Defense housing projects. At the same time, Eero served with the Office of Strategic

General Motors Technical Center (1951–56), Warren, Mich., which received the American Institute of Architects' 25-Year Award in 1985. (Kevin Roche John Dinkeloo and Associates)

Kresge Auditorium (1956), Massachusetts Institute of Technology, Cambridge, Mass. (Calvin Campbell, MIT)

Eero Saarinen. (Kevin Roche John Dinkeloo and Associates)

Kresge Chapel (1956), MIT, a brick cylinder. (Joseph Molitor)

Gateway Arch at the Jefferson National Expansion Memorial (1948), St. Louis, a reverse catenary curve in stainless steel, refined to 630 feet in height. (Seagram County Court House Archives, © Library of Congress)

David S. Ingalls Hockey Rink (1956–59), Yale University, New Haven, Conn. (© Ezra Stoller, ESTO)

John Deere and Company Building (1957–63), Moline, Ill. (John Deere and Company)

Services and exhibited a commitment to industrialization with such projects as his "unfolding-house" as well as a "demountable space" designed in 1942 for U.S. Gypsum and the Pre-Assembled Component (PAC) house designed with Oliver Lundquist.

In 1947 the family partnership was reorganized as Saarinen, Saarinen and Associates, with direction shifting to Eero. Work at Antioch College (1945–49), Yellow Springs, Ohio, the Des Moines Art Center (1944–48, with Brooks-Borg Associated Architects) and Drake University (1946–50), Des Moines, led to an expanding practice. In 1948 Eero, in a submission separate from one by his father, won the Jefferson National Expansion Memorial competition with his Gateway Arch in St. Louis.

At the same time, work had begun on several large-scale projects, including the General Motors Technical Center (1951–56), Warren, Mich. Eero's GMTC aesthetic was based on a resemblance to the pure classic "boxes" in steel, glass and masonry popularized by Ludwig Mies van der Rohe. However, the brick was glazed in bright colors, the technology of the glass curtain wall was itself derived from the rubber gasket installation of automobile wind-shields, and the campus layout was styled after the paradigm of an automotive test track. His curtain-wall aesthetic was sometimes a hard, machinelike element, as in the IBM Manufacturing Plant (1956–59), Rochester, Minn., but also underwent variation in treatment in other projects.

Eero also enlarged his design vocabulary to include a variety of associations and images. For the Kresge Auditorium and the Chapel (both 1956) at the Massachu-

Washington Dulles International Airport (1958–62), Chantilly, Va., embodying a sense of movement and flight. (Balthazar Korab)

CBS Building (1960–64), New York, Saarinen's only tall building and his last design. (Kevin Roche John Dinkeloo and Associates)

setts Institute of Technology, Cambridge, the advanced thin-shell technology in the auditorium dome contrasts with the primal imagery of the chapel's closed brick cylinder placed in a circular sunken moat. The David S. Ingalls Hockey Rink (1956–59) at Yale University, New Haven, Conn., suggests a Viking vessel, its great arch embodying movement, and the complex curvilinear forms of the TWA Terminal at Idlewild (now Kennedy) Airport (1956–62), New York, suggest a hovering bird.

Structure and industrialization remained constants in Eero's search for form. He made use of dramatic mirror glass in the Bell Laboratories (1957–62), Holmdell, N.J., and self-rusting exposed steel framework at the John Deere and Company Building (1957–63), Moline, Ill. Later projects began to exhibit a more refined, pure geometry, seen in the U.S. Embassy (1955–59), Oslo, Norway, a simple triangular building; the CBS Building (1960–64), New York, with its solid, dominating masonry facing; and the Washington Dulles International Airport (1958–62), Chantilly, Va.

Eero's independent career represents only 11 years. He died suddenly of a brain tumor while 10 of his major works were under construction. The firm was succeeded in 1966 by Kevin Roche John Dinkeloo and Associates. In 1962 Eero was posthumously awarded the Gold Medal of the American Institute of Architects. At his death, architectural practice in the service of an institutional and corporate elite came under attack, but his work is of increasing interest in its search to reconcile modern technology and expression with a formal language having the power of communication and allusion. ◮

SKIDMORE, OWINGS AND MERRILL
Albert Bush-Brown

The firm Skidmore, Owings and Merrill (SOM) has created distinctive modern imagery for corporate headquarters and urban areas, all exhibiting the firm's team approach to architectural design, its technical proficiencies and its vast organizational powers. SOM's works have spanned a half century, beginning with the cable-tensioned Travel and Transport Building at the 1933 Chicago Exposition and including the government-commissioned wartime town of Oak Ridge, Tenn. (1942–46), and the dramatic Lever House (1950–52), New York. Although SOM's aesthetic legacy is diverse, partner Fazlur Khan has stated its unifying theme: "Technology is our art form." SOM seeks a marriage of structural support, technical services, sculptural form and spatial sequence so that their unity looks strong and inevitable.

The partnership began in 1936, when Louis Skidmore (1897–1962) and Nathaniel A. Owings (1903–84) began practicing together; in 1949 John O. Merrill (1896–1975) was made a full partner. Ever alert to renewal of talent and to continuity in its command of comprehensive design, the partnership was sequentially enlarged, with Gordon Bunshaft, Walter A. Netsch, Myron Goldsmith, Edward C. Bassett and Bruce J. Graham guiding monumental and distinguished designs from the 1950s well into the 1980s. A third generation, including David Childs, Michael McCarthy, Raul deArmas, James De-Stefano, Adrian Smith and Marc Goldstein, ascended to design major projects from the 1970s on. In the mid-1980s, 47 partners directing more than 1,400 architects, urban planners and interior designers from offices in Chicago, New York, San Francisco, Portland, Washington, D.C., Boston, Los Angeles, Houston and Denver guide national and international projects often costing upwards of $250 million.

Beginning with the urban court and thin slab of the elegantly curtain-walled Lever House and the lighted, glazed box of the Manufacturers Hanover Trust Building (1953–54), SOM/New York perfected the functional and symbolic expression of the office building, achieving elegant expressions in the PepsiCo Incorporated World Headquarters Building (1958–59), Chase Manhattan Bank Building (1957–61), One Liberty Plaza (1963), Marine

Opposite: John O. Merrill, Nathaniel A. Owings and Louis Skidmore. (Courtesy Skidmore, Owings and Merrill)

Rendering of the plan of Oak Ridge, Tenn. (1942–46). (Courtesy Skidmore, Owings and Merrill)

Travel and Transport Building (1933), Century of Progress International Exposition, Chicago, a tensile structure for which Skidmore served as chief of design. (Bill Hedrich, Hedrich-Blessing)

Lever House (1950–52), New York, which set the pattern for the modern office building. It was awarded the American Institute of Architects' 25-Year Award in 1980. (© Ezra Stoller, ESTO)

Beinecke Rare Book and Manuscript Library (1963), Yale University, New Haven, Conn., built of granite-covered trusses filled in with white translucent marble. (T. Charles Erickson, Yale University)

Top and above: U.S. Air Force Academy (1955–59), Colorado Springs, Colo. The chapel is a counterpoint to the rectilinear order of the academic and residential buildings. (Hedrich-Blessing; Stewarts)

Midland Bank (1967) and Park Avenue Plaza (1983). SOM/ Chicago emphasized structural expression in the Inland Steel Building (1958), the John Hancock Center (1970) and the Sears Tower (1974), soaring to 1,470 feet and 109 stories, with 4.4 million square feet. SOM/San Francisco gave the city the faceted Bank of America Building (1969–71), 444 Market Street (1975–81) and the Crocker Center (1982–84).

Responding to the postwar growth of suburban corporate headquarters, SOM designed comprehensive office buildings and industrial parks for Connecticut General Life Insurance Company (1957), Bloomfield, Conn., American Can Company (1970), Greenwich, Conn., Weyerhaeuser Company (1971), Tacoma, Wash., Baxter Travenol (1975), Deerfield, Ill., and Texaco (1977), Harrison, N.Y., among others. New and expanding cultural institutions, defying the earlier bias for historic styles, commissioned SOM to design the U.S. Air Force Academy (1955–59), Colorado Springs, Colo., the University of Illinois at Chicago Circle (1965), the new wing of the Albright-Knox Gallery (1962), Buffalo, and the Beinecke Rare Book and Manuscript Library (1963) at Yale University, New Haven, Conn.

Sears Tower (1974), Chicago, a cluster of framed tubes of varying heights. (© Ezra Stoller, ESTO)

Hirshhorn Museum and Sculpture Garden (1974), Washington, D.C. (Hirshhorn Museum)

Outside the continental United States, SOM designed the Mauna Kea Beach Hotel (1965), on the island of Hawaii, Banque Lambert (1965), Brussels, and the internationally acclaimed tented and cabled Haj Terminal (1982) at the international airport, Jeddah, Saudi Arabia.

In contrast to the pristine calibration found in its 1950s buildings such as Lever House, SOM's buildings of the mid-1980s are richly faceted forms with tubular structures rising from irregular sites and often with combinations of offices, retail shops and residences, as in One Magnificent Mile (1985), Chicago. Concern for urban context has encouraged SOM's designers to relate new forms to neighboring buildings, as in the Federal Reserve Bank Building (1984), San Francisco. The Southwest Financial Center (1985), Miami, and the InterFirst Building (1983), Houston, gave their respective cities urban symbols derived from structural and functional premises, the hallmarks of SOM's architectural practice.

In 1962 SOM won the first Architectural Firm Award of the American Institute of Architects. The AIA also awarded its Gold Medal to two of the original partners—Louis Skidmore in 1957 and Nathaniel Owings in 1983. ◢

LOUIS I. KAHN
John Lobell

Louis Isidore Kahn (1901–74) was born on the Baltic
Island of Saarama, Estonia. His parents brought him as a
child to Philadelphia, where he grew up in a poor Jewish
household. In the 1920s Kahn studied architecture at the
University of Pennsylvania, which embraced the Beaux-
Arts tradition of formal planning and classical revivals.
After graduation, he worked in several offices and traveled
in Europe. In the 1930s he discovered modern architecture
through Le Corbusier's book *Vers une Architecture* (1923),
saying of that time: "I lived in a city called Le Corbusier."

Kahn had difficulty resolving the principles of the
Beaux-Arts with modern architecture, and his early
buildings were undistinguished. He gained a reputation as
a thinker and a theorist, however, teaching architecture at
Yale University from 1947 to 1957 and then at the
University of Pennsylvania from 1957 until his death.

In 1957 Kahn designed the Richards Medical Research
Building at the University of Pennsylvania, Philadelphia,
which quickly gained recognition as a culmination and
extension of modern architecture. In it he expressed not
only the functional requirements of the building's
scientific activities but also their meanings and separated
the "served" from "servant" spaces. He also pressed the
investigation of structure, materials and details to new
levels. Each material, such as brick and concrete, is
articulated and respected for its abilities and traditions,
and that respect is clearly communicated in the design.

In the Salk Institute for Biological Studies, La Jolla,
Calif., begun in 1959, Kahn extended his ideas, applying
them to a concrete building overlooking the Pacific

Louis I. Kahn. (University of Pennsylvania Archives)

Richards Medical Research Building
(1957–61), University of Pennsylvania, Philadelphia, whose exterior
design expresses the building's
functions and complements existing buildings. (© 1979 Cervin
Robinson)

Top and above: Salk Institute for Biological Studies (1959–65), La Jolla, Calif., encompassing a central court flanked by laboratories and offices, with walls angled toward the ocean. The forms and materials reflect the richness of Roman architectural forms. (Both, John Lobell)

Right, below and opposite: Kimbell
Art Museum (1966–72), Fort Worth,
Tex., distinguished by its cycloid
design. Kahn's sketch shows the
high vaulted spaces, used for an
outside court and exhibition galler-
ies, and the lower areas, used for
vestibules and storage. (Kimbell Art
Museum; Kimbell Art Museum;
© 1977 Louis I. Kahn Collection,
University of Pennsylvania and
Pennsylvania Historical and
Museum Commission)

Library (1967–72), Phillips Exeter
Academy, Exeter, N.H. Great circular shapes cut in the concrete
walls allow light inside. (John
Lobell)

Yale Center for British Art and
Studies (1969–74), New Haven,
Conn., a strong concrete grid clad
in pewter-colored stainless steel.
(John Lobell)

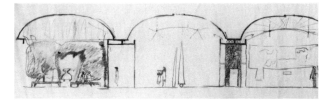

Ocean. In 1962 he began work on a new capital complex for East Pakistan (now Bangladesh), using the meanings of human institutions as an ordering principle. He placed the mosque between the Assembly and the Supreme Court, so that symbolically religion could mediate between the immediate concerns of the legislators and the more philosophical concerns of the justices. He wanted the city to reflect the whole person and so included a sports complex, which symbolized the body, as well as the government buildings, which symbolized the mind. His Kimbell Art Museum (1966–72), Fort Worth, Tex., brought together the viewer and the paintings in natural light. Light also played a major role in his 1967 design of the library for Phillips Exeter Academy, Exeter, N.H.

Kahn's last building was the Yale Center for British Art and Studies (1969–74), New Haven, Conn. The Yale Center sums up the themes in Kahn's work: use of structure as an organizing force, investigation of materials as exploration of the meanings of institutions and the human relationship to natural light.

Kahn is as influential for his philosophy as for his buildings. He used poetic metaphors to describe the architect's role as a bringing of things from the realm of potential, which he called "silence," to the realm of realization, which he called "light." This act is governed by "order," which is the operating principle behind all things. Kahn once said: "A work is made in the urging sounds of industry, and, when the dust settles, the pyramid, echoing Silence, gives the sun its shadow."

Designs did not come easily to Kahn, and he spent long hours struggling over his work. He was often behind schedule and over budget, and because of office inefficiencies he accumulated extensive debts. Overwork, debts and repeated strenuous travel to India and Bangladesh contributed to his death by heart attack during a return trip from India. Despite—or perhaps because of—his struggles, Kahn received recognition as one of the leading architects of modern time. He was awarded the Gold Medal of the American Institute of Architects in 1971 and the Royal Gold Medal for Architecture from the Royal Institute of British Architects in 1972. ◳

Glass House (1949), New Canaan, Conn., inspired in part by Ludwig Mies van der Rohe, who claimed that it was possible to design an all-glass house. (Carleton Knight III)

Philip Johnson in the 1970s. (Carleton Knight III, NTHP)

Museum for Pre-Columbian Art (1963), Dumbarton Oaks, Washington, D.C. Eight of the nine intersecting domed circles are clad entirely in glass so that "the leaves are the walls." (Courtesy Philip Johnson)

PHILIP JOHNSON
Carleton Knight III

By virtue of his more than 50 years in and around the profession, Philip Johnson (1906–) is regarded widely as the dean of contemporary American architects. But architecture's elder statesman shows no signs of slowing down and thus remains, with his rapier sharp wit, its controversial enfant terrible as well. In the past decade—perhaps the busiest of his long career—Johnson, with his partner of two decades, John Burgee, has changed the look of city skylines across the country with a picturesque group of image-making skyscrapers. His recent buildings include Pennzoil Place (1976) in Houston, the Garden Grove Community Church (Crystal Cathedral) (1980) in Garden Grove, Calif., and the American Telephone and Telegraph Company headquarters (1984) in New York, but his influence extends far beyond these.

Johnson, who has said that he always likes "to go against the grain," is equally articulate visually and verbally. As a result, he has had a profound impact on the direction of American architecture over six decades. In the 1930s as an architectural historian, he helped introduce modern architecture—the glass box—to America with a book and exhibit on the International Style at the Museum of Modern Art in New York, where he was director of the architecture department. In the 1940s Johnson the historian became Johnson the architect and built what is perhaps the country's most famous modern house, the Glass House (1949), his own residence in New Canaan, Conn.

In the 1950s he collaborated with Ludwig Mies van der Rohe on the design of the Seagram Building (1954–58), New York, but he began as well to speak out against the purist International Style aesthetic. "You cannot not know history," he told students at Yale University, who had been taught by their devout modernist instructors to ignore the past. In the 1960s Johnson began to invest his modern buildings with historical references, as with the Ottoman Empire–inspired Museum for Pre-Columbian Art (1963) at Dumbarton Oaks, Washington, D.C. Later, joined by partner Burgee, he designed his first highrise office building, the IDS Center, Minneapolis, completed in 1973.

IDS Center (1973), Minneapolis, Johnson and Burgee's first completed high-rise office building, a departure from the glass box concept. (Carleton Knight III)

In the 1970s the man who introduced the glass box became the one to break it, with the Chippendale-pedimented design of the AT&T headquarters, and in so doing he brought professional respectability to Post-Modern architecture, a quality it had failed to achieve previously. Now, in the 1980s, with a growing number of powerful developers as clients, he continues remaking the urban landscape and enhancing his reputation as the most influential architect in the United States. "What's fun in life is change," says Johnson with an impish grin.

As for his place in history, the architect does not consider himself in the same league with such past masters as Mies van der Rohe, Le Corbusier and Frank Lloyd Wright. "I'm not a form-giver," he notes, "but we're not in an age of form-giving. My contribution has been working with younger architects." He once told the *New York Times*, "I'm not creating forms; I'm creating attitudes."

If anything, Johnson is committed to quality in the built environment and to beauty. He collects art with a passion and speaks out frequently in support of historic preservation. Johnson was one of the few persons marching to save New York's Pennsylvania Station in the mid-1960s and lent his name to the successful effort to preserve Grand Central Terminal a decade later. Addressing Mount Holyoke College graduates in 1966, Johnson said, "My favorite Roman emperor, Augustus, used to boast that he had found Rome a city of brick and left it a city of marble. Now we, on the contrary, actually are proud to say that we find a city of stone and brick and are leaving it a city of precast concrete and corrugated tin." By word and by deed, the winner of the 1978 Gold Medal of the American Institute of Architects and, in 1979, the first Pritzker Prize is doing his best to see that this does not happen. ◨

Top and above: Garden Grove Community Church (Crystal Cathedral) (1980), Garden Grove, Calif., a dramatic building sheathed in mirror glass over a white-painted steel frame. The sanctuary, which seats 3,000 persons, opens onto the parking lot to allow a drive-in ministry. (Both, Gordon H. Schenck, Jr.)

Top and above: American Telephone and Telegraph Company Building (1984), New York, whose most prominent identifying feature is its Chippendale pediment. The lobby features the "Spirit of Communication," a golden statue that once topped the old corporate offices. (© 1984 Richard Payne; © 1983 Wolfgang Hoyt, ESTO)

Pennzoil Place (1976), Houston, a pair of trapezoids with sliced-off tops, a project designed to prove that quality architecture could bring a large economic return for developers. (© 1978 Richard Payne)

PPG Place (1984), Pittsburgh, a Gothic-inspired office complex for a glass manufacturer rendered, appropriately, in mirror glass. (© 1984 Richard Payne)

I. M. PEI
Peter Blake

Ioeh Ming Pei (1917–) was born in Canton, China, and educated at the Massachusetts Institute of Technology and Harvard University. Walter Gropius, his principal teacher at Harvard's Graduate School of Design, liked to say that Pei was by far his most promising student and proceeded to make him an assistant professor in 1945, even before Pei had obtained his master's degree. On leaving Harvard in 1948, Pei joined the developer William Zeckendorf and became the director of architecture in Zeckendorf's New York–based firm, Webb and Knapp. He established his own practice in 1955 and has headed the firm of I. M. Pei and Partners ever since.

Pei has designed some of the most important structures built in the second half of the 20th century. His National Center for Atmospheric Research (1961–67), in Boulder, Colo., the Dallas City Hall (1972–77), the East Building of the National Gallery of Art (1978), in Washington, D.C., the John F. Kennedy Library (1979), in Boston, and his innumerable cultural facilities, office buildings, housing complexes, university buildings, research facilities and urban centers have been invariably self-assured and elegant. Perhaps more important, they have often been on the leading edge of aesthetic, technological and urban innovation. Pei, more than any of his contemporaries, has taken the diagrams of the modern pioneers and translated them into reality.

He is probably the first to have used exposed, cast-in-place and precast concrete in modern, multistory housing, refining it in detail and finish so that a Pei-designed exposed concrete building looks as polished as a slab of marble. He has been the most daring pioneer in the United States in the development of all-glass curtain walls, encountering serious problems along the way, but surmounting them to produce some of the most beautiful structures in that idiom since the Crystal Palace. And he has done innovative work in the use of space frames and other advanced structural and mechanical systems.

Even more important, perhaps, have been Pei's efforts to turn each new urban project into an opportunity to strengthen the urban fabric as a whole. Pei realized that

Opposite: National Center for Atmospheric Research (1961–67), Boulder, Colo., a pioneer work in concrete technology recalling the region's pueblo heritage. (© Ezra Stoller, ESTO)

I. M. Pei (Evelyn Hofer, I. M. Pei and Partners)

Opposite: Dallas City Hall (1972–77), a concrete trapezoidal building with a cantilevered facade. The long, low structure embraces the plaza. (Frank Branger)

Mile High Center (U.S. National Bank of Denver) (1955), Denver, a commercial center with generous urban spaces that sparked a major downtown revival. (© Ezra Stoller, ESTO)

Below, middle and opposite: East Building (1978), National Gallery of Art, Washington, D.C., a dramatic marble structure based on a trapezoidal module and lighted by a skylight incorporating the same forms. The aerial view shows the structure's relationship to the original gallery and the U.S. Capitol. (© Ezra Stoller, ESTO; Robert Lautman; © Ezra Stoller, ESTO)

John F. Kennedy Library (1979), Boston, reflecting the creative arrangement of masses that is a hallmark of Pei's architecture. (Nathaniel Lieberman)

urban design in a free-enterprise society, where social and political controls tend to be loose, would demand considerable diplomatic as well as architectural skills. Thus, most of Pei's urban projects have been architectural as well as diplomatic accomplishments. In Montreal, for example, the design of a single center—Place Ville Marie (1962)—became the opening wedge for a major effort to transform the pedestrian and mass transit patterns of the city's core. In Dallas the design of the city hall generated significant new urban spaces and pedestrian linkages. And in Denver, the Mile High Center (1955), Hilton Hotel and surrounding stores and open spaces have generated a major renewal of an aging city center. The American Institute of Architects gave its 1968 Architectural Firm Award to I. M. Pei and Partners and its 1979 Gold Medal to Pei himself.

Two of Pei's latest projects illustrate the growth of his ideas. The Bank of China Tower in Hong Kong (1983–, with the structural engineer Leslie Robertson) will be more than 1,000 feet tall, and its triangulated structure will be radically different from that of any skyscraper built. The new addition to the Louvre in Paris, with its widely publicized glass pyramid designed to serve as the main entrance, is, in fact, a vast subterranean complex of services and passages that is intended to make the Louvre complex, for the first time, an integral and accessible part of modern Paris.

In short, Pei's preoccupation with technological and aesthetic innovation and urban integration continues to set him apart from contemporaries whose concern tends to be the single building. His work is not an isolated event but a continuous effort to enhance our cities and to make them more cohesive and expressive of our culture. ◣

VENTURI, RAUCH AND SCOTT BROWN
John Andrew Gallery

When Robert Venturi (1925–) wrote *Complexity and Contradiction in Architecture* in 1966, he advocated a theory of architecture radically different from concepts that had prevailed in the United States since the introduction of the International Style in the 1920s. The writings and works of Venturi and his partners, John Rauch (1930–) and Denise Scott Brown (1931–), have often outraged the architectural profession but in the process have transformed contemporary architecture more than those of any other American firm.

Venturi was born in Philadelphia, the son of a wholesale fruit grocer, and from the age of four knew he wanted to be an architect. He studied at Princeton University, where recognition of the International Style as only one of a long series of architectural styles allowed him to develop his love of architectural history and discover the work of many architects rejected by the modern movement. As recipient of the 1954 Prix de Rome, Venturi further developed his interest in historic styles, drawing particularly on the work of Michelangelo, Palladio and the Italian Mannerists. On returning from Rome, Venturi worked for Louis Kahn and taught at the University of Pennsylvania, where he met his future wife and partner, Scott Brown. He collaborated with Cope and Lippincott on several projects before establishing a partnership with William Short in 1960 and then with John Rauch in 1964.

Rauch studied art at Wesleyan University, where he developed a love of architectural history that made him dissatisfied with contemporary design, and later he studied architecture at the University of Pennsylvania. While working at Cope and Lippincott he gravitated to Venturi, whose ideas and enthusiasms were in marked contrast to those of many established architects.

Scott Brown grew up in South Africa, where her mother was an architect, and was educated there and in England. She came to the United States to study architecture and planning at the University of California at Berkeley and the University of Pennsylvania and joined Venturi's firm in 1967. Her exposure to the work of

Guild House (1960–63, with Cope and Lippincott), Philadelphia, Friends' housing for the elderly. (William Watkins)

Opposite: John Rauch, Denise Scott Brown and Robert Venturi. (Matt Wargo)

Herbert Gans reinforced her ideas on social planning, popular culture and vernacular urban form, all of which fit well with Venturi's architectural theories and led to the book *Learning from Las Vegas* (1971).

In contrast to most modern architects, Venturi, Rauch and Scott Brown have not attempted to develop a particular style that is repeated from one building to the next. Their work is based on certain architectural concepts expressed in unusual terms: a desire to produce buildings that are "ugly and ordinary" and buildings that are "decorated sheds." During the first 10 years of the firm's existence, these architectural ideas were so radical that work was difficult to obtain. Most of the early work consisted of small buildings, such as the Fire Station No. 4 (1965–67), Columbus, Ind., and houses, such as the Vanna Venturi House (1962), Philadelphia. Only in recent years, with the broader acceptance of their theories, have the architects obtained larger commissions.

A primary starting point for all their buildings is the immediate context: local materials, forms and building traditions. At first glance, their houses in Bermuda, Nantucket and Delaware look ordinary, like other houses in the area; at second glance it becomes apparent that local elements are used in a highly distinctive manner and combined with a variety of historical references, ornamentation and invention. Exterior facades are often treated as independent decoration using color and patterns in the materials themselves.

Although they draw on a variety of historical references, Venturi, Rauch and Scott Brown are American architects, perhaps the most influential since Frank Lloyd Wright. In 1985 the firm won the Architectural Firm Award of the American Institute of Architects. Their work has been the basis for the current eclectic design attitudes of the Post-Modern movement and continues to challenge architectural theory and practice around the world. ◩

Vanna Venturi House (1962), Chestnut Hill, Philadelphia, a stucco structure from Venturi's "classical" period. (Rollin La France)

Franklin Court (1976), Philadelphia, featuring a "ghost" of Ben Franklin's house, all that could be reconstructed accurately from archeological evidence. (Steven Shore, Mark Cohn)

Trubek-Wislocki Houses (1970), Nantucket, Mass., shingle structures whose design recalls early New England saltbox houses. (Steven Izenour)

Addition (1973), Allen Memorial Art Museum, Oberlin College, Oberlin, Ohio, a multicolored tile extension of a Beaux-Arts building. (Oberlin College)

Faculty Club (1974), Pennsylvania State University, State College, Pa., a
long, low building reminiscent of the Shingle Style. (Tom Bernard)

Middle and above: Gordon Wu Hall
(1980), Butler College, Princeton
University, Princeton, N.J., a modern building incorporating some
Gothic elements of other campus
buildings. The geometric pattern on
the facade is symbolic of gate
patterns at Cambridge and Oxford
universities. (Tom Bernard)

More Historic American Architects

The following catalog presents other notable historic American architects whose work is frequently cited and appreciated. The catalog is meant to be a quick reference to aid in finding basic information about a larger number of architects than could be presented in the main essays; more detailed information can be found in the sources included in the reading list. Among the items highlighted are the primary place of business, other architects with whom the person was associated at one time and a selection of representative projects.

AUSTIN, HENRY (1804–91). New Haven, Conn. Associated with Ithiel Town. Noted for his work in the Italian villa and oriental styles. Yale College Library (Dwight Memorial Chapel) (1842–45), Grove Street Cemetery Gate (1849), first railroad station (1849), City Hall (1862), New Haven, Conn.; Morse-Libby House (1859–63), Portland, Maine.

BACON, HENRY (1866–1924). New York. Associated with McKim, Mead and White. Specialized in commemorative buildings and public monuments. Awarded AIA Gold Medal in 1923. Lincoln Memorial (1911–22), Washington, D.C.

BADGER, DANIEL D. (1806–84). New York. Innovator in cast iron and architectural ironwork. Haughwout Store (1856), New York; Watervliet Arsenal (1859), near Troy, N.Y.

BENJAMIN, ASHER (1773–1845). Boston. Wrote seven pattern books that helped disseminate Georgian, Federal and Greek Revival styles. Charles Street Meetinghouse (1807), Boston.

BOGARDUS, JAMES (1800–74). New York. Awarded patent for first complete iron building. Laing Stores (1848), Harper and Brothers Printing Plant (1854), New York.

BREUER, MARCEL (1902–81). Berlin, England and New York. Bauhaus-trained; partner of Walter Gropius; influenced architects and furniture designers; educator. Awarded AIA Gold Medal in 1968. Unesco Secretariat Building and Conference Hall (1953–58, with Pier Luigi Nervi and Bernard Zehrfuss), Paris; Whitney Museum of American Art (1966), New York; U.S. Department of Housing and Urban Development (1963–68), Washington, D.C.

BUCKLAND, WILLIAM (1734–74). Virginia and Maryland. Designed elaborate interiors and woodwork. Gunston Hall (1755–59), Lorton, Va.; Mount Airy (1761–64), Richmond County, Va.; Chase-Lloyd House (1773), Hammond-Harwood House (1774), Annapolis, Md.

CARRÈRE AND HASTINGS (1885–1915). John Merven Carrère (1858–1911) and Thomas Hastings (1860–1929). New York. Specialized in Beaux-Arts designs. Ponce de Leon Hotel (1888), St. Augustine, Fla.; New York Public Library (1902–11), Manhattan Bridge and Approaches (1904–11), Henry Clay Frick House (1914), Standard Oil Building (1926), New York.

COBB, HENRY IVES (1859–1931). Chicago. Known for personalized adaptations of Romanesque and Gothic styles. Fisheries Building (1893), World's Columbian Exposition; plan for the University of Chicago (1895), Chicago.

COPE AND STEWARDSON (1885–1902). Walter Cope (1860–1902) and John Stewardson (1858–96). Philadelphia. Known for campus designs and buildings in the Collegiate Gothic style. Buildings at Bryn Mawr College (1886–1904) and the University of Pennsylvania (1895–1901), Philadelphia; Princeton University (1895–1903), Princeton, N.J.; Washington University (1899–1905), St. Louis.

CRET, PAUL PHILIPPE (1876–1945). Philadelphia. Modern classicist and educator. Awarded AIA Gold Medal in 1938. Indianapolis Public Library (1914–17, with Zantzinger, Borie and Medary); Delaware River Bridge (1920–26, with Ralph Modjeski), Philadelphia; Detroit Institute of Arts (1919–27, with Zantzinger, Borie and Medary); Folger Shakespeare Library (1928–32), Washington, D.C.

DAKIN, JAMES H. (1806–52). New York and Louisiana. Associated with Town and Davis. Specialized in Greek, Gothic and Egyptian Revival works. New York University (1833–37), New York; Bank of Louisville (1836); Louisiana State Capitol (1847–52), Baton Rouge.

DELANO AND ALDRICH (1903–41). William Adams Delano (1874–1960) and Chester Holmes Aldrich (1871–1940). New York. Delano awarded AIA Gold Medal in 1953. Designed estates for wealthy owners. Walters Art Gallery (1910), Baltimore; John D. Rockefeller House (1906–08), Pocantico Hills, N.Y.; La Guardia Air Terminal (1940), New York.

EAMES, CHARLES (1907–78). St. Louis and California. Worked closely with wife, Ray Kaiser Eames, and Eero Saarinen in many media including furniture design, exhibits and film. Charles Eames Residence (Case Study House No. 8 for *Arts and Architecture*) (1945–49, with Eero Saarinen), John Entenza Residence (Case Study House No. 9) (1945–50, with Eero Saarinen), Pacific Palisades, Calif; Herman Miller Showroom (1947–49), Beverly Hills, Calif.

EBERSON, JOHN (1875–1954). St. Louis. Introduced flamboyant, atmospheric ("stars and clouds") design in 100 American movie theaters. Majestic Theater (1922), Houston; Avalon and Paradise theaters (1928), Chicago; Paradise Theater, Bronx, N.Y.; Loew's State Theater (1928), Louisville.

EIDLITZ, LEOPOLD (1823–1908). New York. Proponent of Gothic designs and structuralism. New York State Capitol (1875–85, with H. H. Richardson and Frederick Law Olmsted), Albany; County "Tweed" Courthouse (southern wing) (1878), New York.

FLAGG, ERNEST (1857–1947). New York. Practitioner of the Beaux-Arts and reformer focusing on zoning and small houses. Corcoran Gallery of Art (1892–97), Washington, D.C.; Singer Building (1896–99) and Tower (1908), New York; U.S. Naval Academy (1896–1908), Annapolis, Md.

FULLER, R. BUCKMINSTER (1895–1983). Illinois. Architectural and technological innovator and designer of geodesic domes. Awarded AIA Gold Medal in 1970. Dymaxion House (1927); U.S. Air Force DEW (Distant Early Warning) Line dome radar shelters (1954), Arctic Circle; U.S. Pavilion, 1967 International Exposition, Montreal.

GALLIER, JAMES, SR. (1798–1866). New Orleans. Partner of Minard Lafever, Charles B. Dakin and James H. Dakin. Leading Greek Revival architect in New Orleans. Government Street Presbyterian Church (1835), Mobile; Merchants Exchange (1835), Saint Charles Hotel (1836), City Hall (Gallier Hall) (1845–50), New Orleans.

GEDDES, NORMAN BEL (1893–1958). New York. Prolific theater designer and stager who later specialized in streamlined industrial design and interiors. General Motors (Futurama) Exhibition (1939), New York World's Fair.

GOFF, BRUCE (1904–82). Chicago and Oklahoma. Innovator who combined late Prairie School principles with expressive responses to clients' individual preferences, specializing in houses. Libbey-Owens-Ford Showroom (1937), Merchandise Mart, Chicago; Bartman House (Triaero) (1941), near Fern Creek, Ky.; Military Chapel (1945), Camp Parks, Calif.; Bavinger House (1950–55), near Norman, Okla.; Price House (1956–78), Bartlesville, Okla.

GRIFFIN, MARION MAHONY (1871–1962). Chicago and Australia. Served as a draftsman for Frank Lloyd Wright; later teamed with husband, Walter B. Griffin. Known for renderings and interior features. Ceiling, Capitol Theatre (1924), Melbourne; Castlecrag Community (1921–35), Sydney.

GRIFFIN, WALTER BURLEY (1876–1937). Midwest and Australia. Worked with Frank Lloyd Wright. Adherent of Prairie School principles and comprehensive community and landscape planning. W. H. Emery House (1902), Elmhurst, Ill.; J. G. Melson House (1912), Mason City, Iowa; Stinson Memorial Library (1912–14), Anna, Ill.; city plan (1912), Canberra; Capitol Theatre (1924), Melbourne; Castlecrag Community (1921–35), Sydney.

GRUEN, VICTOR (1903–80). Vienna, New York and Los Angeles. Planner who specialized in large suburban shopping centers. Northland Center (1954), Detroit; Southdale Shopping Center (1956), Minneapolis; Midtown Plaza (1962), Rochester, N.Y.; Sea World (1966), San Diego.

HADFIELD, GEORGE (1763–1826). Washington, D.C. Superintended construction of the U.S. Capitol, 1795–98; Custis-Lee Mansion (1802–04, 1817), Arlington, Va.; Old City Hall (1820–26), Washington, D.C.

HARRISON AND ABRAMOVITZ (1945–78). Wallace K. Harrison (1895–1981) and Max Abramovitz (1908–). New York. Worked as part of larger teams on major 20th-century urban projects. Harrison awarded AIA Gold Medal in 1967. Rockefeller Center (1929–33, 1941–74, with Raymond Hood et al.), Perisphere and Trylon (1939–40), New York World's Fair, United Nations Building (1947–53), Avery Fisher Hall (1959–62), Metropolitan Opera House (1962–66), New York. Harrison, South Mall (1963–78), Albany, N.Y.

HARRISON, PETER (1716–75). Newport, R.I., Boston and Cambridge, Mass. One of the first colonial architects to use Palladian precepts. Redwood Library (1750), Touro Synagogue (1759–63), Brick Market (1761–73), Newport, R.I.; King's Chapel (1749–58), Boston.

HAYDEN, SOPHIA (1869–1953). The first woman to graduate from MIT's architecture program, in 1890. Woman's Building (1893), World's Columbian Exposition, Chicago.

HOBAN, JAMES (1762–1831). Washington, D.C. Competition winner for the White House (1792–1801), superintendent of construction, U.S. Capitol, 1793–1802, Washington, D.C.

HOLABIRD AND ROCHE (1883–1927). William Holabird (1854–1923) and Martin Roche (1853–1927). Chicago. Trained with William Le Baron Jenney. Influenced the pioneer era of Chicago office building and designed midwestern hotels. Tacoma Building (1889), Old Colony Building (1894, with Corydon T. Purdy), Marquette Building (1895, with Purdy), Chicago Building (1904), La Salle Hotel (1908–09), Chicago.

HOOD, RAYMOND M. (1881–1934). New York. Executed landmark, forward-looking skyscrapers. Chicago Tribune Tower (1923–25, with John Mead Howells), Chicago; Daily News Building (1929–31, with Howells), Rockefeller Center (1930–33, with Reinhard, Hofmeister, Corbett, Harrison, McMurray and Fouilhoux), McGraw-Hill Building (1931, with Godley and Fouilhoux), New York.

HOWARD, JOHN GALEN (1864–1931). San Francisco. Apprenticed with H. H. Richardson and McKim, Mead and White. Designer in classical styles; educator. Executed plan for the University of California (1901–23), Berkeley.

KAHN, ALBERT (1869–1942). Detroit. Innovative industrial designer who tailored factories to new assembly-line engineering needs. Ford Motor Company, River Rouge Plant (1917–39), Dearborn, Mich.; General Motors Building (1922), Detroit; Chrysler Corporation Half-Ton Truck Plant and Export Building (1938), Warren, Mich.; George N. Pierce Plant (1906), Buffalo, N.Y.

LAFEVER, MINARD (1798–1854). New York. Author of popular builders' guides that disseminated the Greek Revival nationwide and designer of numerous churches. Sailors' Snug Harbor (1831–33), Staten Island, N.Y.; New Dutch South Reformed Church (1840), New York; Church of the Holy Trinity (1844–47), Brooklyn, N.Y.

LAMB, THOMAS W. (1871–1942). New York. Dean of the "standard" ("hard-top") school of movie theater design, producing 300 theaters. Capitol Theater (1919), New York; Fox Theater (1929), San Francisco; Loew's State Theater (1929), Syracuse, N.Y.

L'ENFANT, PIERRE CHARLES (1754–1825). Philadelphia. Influenced American city planning and development of Federal-style architecture. Federal Hall remodeling (1789), New York; plan for Washington, D.C. (1791).

LESCAZE AND HOWE (1929–35). William E. Lescaze (1896–1969) and George Howe (1886–1955). Philadelphia. Introduced the International Style to America. Philadelphia Savings Fund Society Building (1931), Philadelphia; Lescaze House (1934), New York.

McINTIRE, SAMUEL (1757–1811). Salem, Mass. Carpenter and builder who excelled in ornamental woodwork. Derby Summer House (1794), Danvers, Mass.; John Gardner House (1805), South Congregational Church (1805), Salem.

MEIGS, MONTGOMERY C. (1816–92). Washington, D.C. U.S. Army engineer and architect. Washington Aqueduct (1852–60), supervising engineer for U.S. Capitol extension (dome and wings), 1852–60, Pension Building (1882–87), Washington, D.C.

NOTMAN, JOHN (1810–65). Philadelphia. Helped introduce the Italianate style and advanced technology. Laurel Hill Cemetery (1836–39), The Athenaeum (1845–47), Philadelphia; Prospect Villa (1852), Princeton, N.J.

PARRIS, ALEXANDER (1780–1852). Boston. Neoclassical builder-architect associated with Bulfinch and others. Governor's Residence (1812), Richmond, Va.; Charlestown Navy Yard and Harbor (dry dock and sea walls) (1819–29), Quincy Market (1823–26), Boston.

PEABODY AND STEARNS (1870–1917). Robert Swain Peabody (1845–1917) and John Goddard Stearns, Jr. (1843–1917). Boston. Prolific and prominent architectural firm that trained numerous young architects. Park Square (Providence) Railroad Station (1874), Mutual Life Insurance Company of New York (1875), Custom House Tower (1909–11), Boston; Kragsyde (1884), Manchester-by-the-Sea, Mass.; Groton School (1886–1901), Groton, Mass.

POPE, JOHN RUSSELL (1874–1937). New York. Known for distinguished classical buildings. National Archives (1933–35), National Gallery of Art (1937–41), Jefferson Memorial (1937–43), Washington, D.C.

POST, GEORGE B. (1837–1913). New York. A leader in the design of early skyscrapers and classical revival commercial buildings. Awarded AIA Gold Medal in 1911. Equitable Life Assurance Company (1868–70), New York Stock Exchange (1901–04), New York; Erie County Savings Bank (1890–94), Buffalo, N.Y.; Manufacturers and Liberal Arts Building (1893), World's Columbian Exposition, Chicago; Wisconsin State Capitol (1904–07), Madison.

POTTER, EDWARD T. (1831–1904). New York. Specialized in High Victorian Gothic churches and colleges. Mark Twain House (1873–81, with Alfred H. Thorp), Hartford, Conn.

POTTER, WILLIAM A. (1842–1909). New York. A supervising architect of the Treasury Department who also designed suburban estates and collegiate buildings. Chancellor Green Library (1873), Princeton University, Princeton, N.J.; South Congregational Church (1872–75), Springfield, Mass.; Customhouse and Post Office (1875–79), Evansville, Ind.

PRICE, BRUCE (1845–1903). New York. Designed Shingle Style houses that influenced Frank Lloyd Wright and others. Tuxedo Park (1885–90), N.Y.; Chateau Frontenac Hotel (1893), Quebec, Canada.

PURCELL AND ELMSLIE (1913–22). William Gray Purcell (1880–1965) and George Grant Elmslie (1871–1952). Minneapolis. Associated with Louis Sullivan. Produced numerous Prairie School landmarks, small, ornamented banks, and Arts and Crafts houses. Merchants Bank (1912, with George Feick), Winona, Minn.; Woodbury County Courthouse (1915–17, with William L. Steele), Sioux City, Iowa; Harold Bradley House (1911), Woods Hole, Mass.; E. W. Decker House (1913), Holdridge, Minn.

REED AND STEM (1889–1911). Charles A. Reed (1857–1911) and Allen H. Stem (1856–1931). St. Paul, Minn., and New York. Designed more than 100 railroad stations. Grand Central Terminal (1903–13, with Warren and Wetmore), New York.

ROEBLING, JOHN AUGUSTUS (1806–69), and WASHINGTON AUGUSTUS ROEBLING (1837–1926). Trenton, N.J. Pioneering suspension bridge engineers. Brooklyn Bridge (1869–83), New York.

ROGERS, ISAIAH (1800–69). Boston, New York and Cincinnati. Innovative hotel designer, inventor and supervising architect of the Treasury Department. Tremont House (1829), Boston; Merchants' Exchange (1836–42), New York; Burnet House (1850), Cincinnati; Treasury Department (west wing) (1865), Washington, D.C.

SCHINDLER, RUDOLPH M. (1887–1953). Los Angeles. Known for International Style houses, use of concrete and cubistic designs. Schindler House (1922), Buck House (1934), Los Angeles; Lovell Beach House (1926), Newport Beach, Calif.

SERT, JOSEP LLUIS (1902–83). Cambridge, Mass. International city and housing pioneer; established urban design program at Harvard University. Awarded AIA Gold Medal in 1981. Spanish Pavilion (1937), World's Fair, Paris; plan for Bogata, Colombia (1951, with Le Corbusier); Peabody Terrace Married Students Housing (1963–65), Harvard University, Cambridge, Mass.

SHAW, HOWARD VAN DOREN (1869–1926). Chicago. Designer of fashionable houses in the Midwest, many in English revival styles. Awarded AIA Gold Medal in 1927. Ragdale (1898), Market Square (1915–16), Lake Forest, Ill.

SHEPLEY, RUTAN AND COOLIDGE (1886–1914). George Foster Shepley (1860–1903), Charles H. Rutan (1851–1914) and Charles A. Coolidge (1858–1936). Brookline, Mass. Successor firm to H. H. Richardson. Stanford University (1892), Stanford, Calif.; Ames Building (1892), Boston; Art Institute of Chicago (1897), Chicago.

SLOAN, SAMUEL (1815–84). Philadelphia. Author of numerous plan books, publisher and designer of public buildings, schools, hospitals for the insane and churches. Alabama Insane (Bryce) Hospital (1852), Tuscaloosa, Ala.; Longwood (1860–62), Natchez, Miss.

SMITHMEYER AND PELZ (1873–88). John L. Smithmeyer (1832–1908) and Paul J. Pelz (1841–1918). Washington, D.C. Designers in classical styles; Pelz also known for lighthouses. Library of Congress (1873–92), Washington, D.C.

STEIN, CLARENCE S. (1883–1975). New York. Proponent of garden cities and planned housing. Awarded AIA Gold Medal in 1956. Radburn, N.J. (1929, with Henry Wright).

STONE, EDWARD DURRELL (1902–78). New York. An International Style designer who evolved a personal idiom noted for the use of marble. Museum of Modern Art (1939, with Philip Goodwin), New York; U.S. Embassy (1954), New Delhi; John F. Kennedy Center for the Performing Arts (1969), Washington, D.C.

TOWN, ITHIEL (1784–1844). New Haven, Conn., and New York. Associated with Alexander J. Davis. Early leader in Greek and Gothic Revival styles and bridge engineering. Trinity Church (1813–16), Connecticut State House (1827–31), New Haven, Conn.; City Hall and Market House (1828–29), Hartford, Conn.; Indiana State Capitol (1831–35, with Davis), Indianapolis; North Carolina State Capitol (1833–40, with Davis et al.), Raleigh.

VAN ALEN, WILLIAM (1883–1954). New York. Designer of the most renowned Art Deco skyscraper. Chrysler Building (1929), New York.

VAN BRUNT, HENRY (1832–1903). Boston and Kansas City, Mo. Associated with William R. Ware and Frank Howe. Key post–Civil War architect and theorist. Memorial Hall (1865–78), Harvard University, Cambridge, Mass.; Coates House Hotel (1889–90), Kansas City.

VAUX, CALVERT (1824–95). Newburgh, N.Y., and New York. Associated with Andrew Jackson Downing and Frederick Law Olmsted. Major early landscape architect, author and designer of cottages and public buildings. Central Park (1858–76, with Olmsted), New York; landscaping, Gallaudet College (1866), Washington, D.C.; Prospect Park and Brooklyn Park System (1866–73), Brooklyn, N.Y.; Samuel J. Tilden House (1881–84), New York; landscaping, Greystone (1880), Yonkers, N.Y.

WARREN AND WETMORE (c. 1900–30). Whitney Warren (1864–1943) and Charles D. Wetmore (1867–1941). New York. Known for hotel designs and railroad buildings. New York Yacht Club (1898), Grand Central Terminal (1903–13, with Reed and Stem), Biltmore Hotel (1914), New York.

WITHERS, FREDERICK C. (1828–1901). Newburgh, N.Y. Associated with Andrew Jackson Downing, Calvert Vaux and Frederick Law Olmsted. Leading designer of High Victorian Gothic architecture and churches. Dutch Reformed Church (1859), Beacon, N.Y.; Gallaudet College (1866–85), Washington, D.C.; Jefferson Market Courthouse (1874–78), Chapel of the Good Shepherd (1888), New York.

WRIGHT, LLOYD (1890–1978). Los Angeles. Trained with father at Oak Park studio; associated with Olmsted and Olmsted and Irving Gill. Landscape architect and designer of precast concrete houses. Hollywood Bowl (first shell, 1924–25; second shell, 1928); Swedenborg Memorial Chapel (Wayfarer's Chapel) (1946–71), Palos Verdes, Calif.

YOUNG, AMMI B. (1798–1874). First supervising architect of the Treasury Department and designer of classical and Italianate public buildings. Vermont State House (1836), Montpelier; Customhouse (1837–47), Boston; Wentworth Hall (1828), Reed Hall (1839), Dartmouth College, Hanover, N.H.; Customhouse and Post Office (1858), Windsor, Vt.

Contributors

Paul R. Baker is professor of history and director of the American civilization program at New York University. A specialist in American intellectual and cultural history, he is author of *Richard Morris Hunt*, among other books.

William L. Beiswanger is the architectural historian at Monticello, Charlottesville, Va., where his responsibilities include documenting the design and construction of Monticello as well as developing and coordinating a program for the restoration and re-creation of Thomas Jefferson's landscape.

Peter Blake, FAIA, is chairman of the Department of Architecture and Planning, the Catholic University of America, Washington, D.C., and maintains an architectural practice in New York. Recipient of the 1975 Architecture Critic's Medal of the American Institute of Architects, he is also author of *The Master Builders: Le Corbusier, Mies van der Rohe, Frank Lloyd Wright; God's Own Junkyard;* and *Form Follows Fiasco—Why Modern Architecture Hasn't Worked.*

Sara Holmes Boutelle, an architectural historian, is a founder of the Julia Morgan Association and is working on a book on Morgan. She lives in Santa Cruz, Calif.

H. Allen Brooks is professor of fine arts at the University of Toronto and has been visiting professor at universities in the United States and at the Architectural Association in London. His books include *Writings on Wright, Frank Lloyd Wright and the Prairie School* and *The Prairie School*, which received the 1972 Alice Davis Hitchcock Book Award. A past president of the Society of Architectural Historians, he also writes extensively on Le Corbusier and is general editor of the 32-volume *Le Corbusier Archive.*

John M. Bryan is associate professor of art history and director of the applied art history program at the University of South Carolina, Columbia. An associate editor of the papers of Robert Mills, he is also writing a biography of Mills.

Albert Bush-Brown, Hon. AIA, has had a long career in university teaching and administration and as consultant for large building projects in the United States and abroad. He is author of *Skidmore, Owings and Merrill: Architecture and Urbanism, 1973–1983* and coauthor of *The Architecture of America: A Social and Cultural History.*

Alson Clark teaches at the School of Architecture at the University of Southern California, Los Angeles, where he has served as head of the Architecture and Fine Arts Library and as professor of the architectural history of southern California.

Jeffrey A. Cohen, a doctoral candidate in art history at the University of Pennsylvania, Philadelphia, is associate editor for architectural history of the papers of Benjamin H. Latrobe, to be published by Yale University Press.

Donald W. Curl is professor of history at Florida Atlantic University, Boca Raton, and author of *Mizner's Florida: American Resort Architecture.*

Jane B. Davies has studied the work, drawings and papers of Alexander J. Davis for more than 25 years. A former Columbia University librarian, she has lectured and published many articles about Davis and is writing a book on his life and work.

Robert B. Ennis teaches the history of art and architecture in the architecture department at Drexel University, Philadelphia. He has conducted research for several years on the life and works of Thomas U. Walter, most recently under the sponsorship of The Athenaeum of Philadelphia.

James Marston Fitch, Hon. AIA, is director of historic preservation for Beyer Blinder Belle, Architects and Planners, in New York. He was for many years a friend of Walter Gropius and is author of *Walter Gropius*, the first biography of him to appear in English. A former director of the historic preservation program at Columbia University, New York, he is author of *American Building: The Environmental Forces That Shape It* and *American Building: The Historical Forces That Shaped It*.

John Andrew Gallery is a principal of Urban Partners, a development consulting firm in Philadelphia. He is editor of *Philadelphia Architecture* and coauthor of *Man-Made Philadelphia*.

David Gebhard is professor of architectural history at the University of California, Santa Barbara, and curator of the Architectural Drawings Collection of the University Art Museum. He is coauthor of *Architecture in Los Angeles: A Complete Guide*, *A Guide to Architecture in San Francisco and Northern California* and *Two Hundred Years of American Architectural Drawings* and is currently working on a book on Irving J. Gill (with Bruce Kamerling).

C. M. Harris is editor of the papers of William Thornton, a two-volume edition of correspondence, writings and drawings to be published by the University Press of Virginia. He is also working on a biography of Thornton and resides in Washington, D.C.

Thomas S. Hines is a professor in the Department of History and School of Architecture and Urban Planning, University of California, Los Angeles. He is author of *Burnham of Chicago: Architect and Planner* and *Richard Neutra and the Search for Modern Architecture*.

Bruce Kamerling is curator of collections for the San Diego Historical Society. The guest curator for a 1979 Irving Gill exhibit at the San Diego Museum of Art, he is currently working on a book on Gill (with David Gebhard).

Harold Kirker is professor of history at the University of California, Santa Barbara, with a special interest in American cultural history. He is author of *The Architecture of Charles Bulfinch* and *California's Architectural Frontier* and coauthor of *Bulfinch's Boston, 1787–1817*.

Carleton Knight III, former editor of *Preservation News*, writes on architecture for a variety of publications and is a contributing editor of *Architecture*. The recipient of a fellowship from the National Endowment for the Arts to study the relationship between architects and their clients, he lives in Washington, D.C.

Antoinette J. Lee is an architectural and urban historian in Washington, D.C., specializing in the design and location of public buildings. She is currently working on a history of the office of the supervising architect of the Treasury Department, which will include a major section on Alfred B. Mullett. She is also a preservation consultant.

Roger K. Lewis, AIA, is associate professor in the School of Architecture, University of Maryland, College Park, and a practicing architect in Washington, D.C. He is author of *Architect? A Candid Guide to the Profession* and writes on architecture and urban design for the *Washington Post*.

John Lobell, an architect living in New York, is professor of architecture at the Pratt Institute, where he teaches history, theory, technology and design. He is author of *Between Silence and Light: Spirit in the Architecture of Louis I. Kahn*, as well as numerous articles and reviews.

Richard Longstreth is associate professor of architectural history and director of the graduate historic preservation program at the George Washington University, Washington, D.C. He is also author of *On the Edge of the World: Four Architects in San Francisco at the Turn of the Century* and chairman of the Society of Architectural Historians' Committee on Preservation and serves on the board of Preservation Action.

W. Ray Luce has been fascinated by octagons since first seeing one in Monroeville, Ohio, and has been collecting material on them for 15 years. A former historian with the National Register of Historic Places, he is the Ohio state historic preservation officer and chief of the historic preservation division, Ohio Historical Society.

Randell L. Makinson, an architect, teacher, historian and preservationist, is director of the Gamble House and the Greene and Greene Library, Pasadena, Calif. He is author of *Greene and Greene: Architecture as a Fine Art* and *Greene and Greene: Furniture and Related Designs*.

Patricia Murphy wrote her master's thesis on Cass Gilbert's early career and served as curator for a touring exhibit of his early works sponsored by the University of Minnesota Gallery. Her projects as a historic preservation consultant and architectural historian have included a citywide survey of St. Paul and a state-owned building survey sponsored by the Minnesota Historical Society. She now resides in Los Angeles.

Paul F. Norton is professor of art history at the University of Massachusetts, Amherst. He has written extensively on Benjamin H. Latrobe as well as other architects, and his books include *Latrobe, Jefferson and the National Capitol*. A former editor of the *Journal of the Society of Architectural Historians*, he is also editor of the papers of Samuel McIntire.

Jeffrey Karl Ochsner, AIA, is author of *H. H. Richardson: Complete Architectural Works* and lecturer in the School of Architecture at Rice University, Houston. He is also a practicing architect in Houston, specializing in urban design and planning.

James F. O'Gorman is Grace Slack McNeil Professor of American Art at Wellesley College, Wellesley, Mass. A past president of the Society for Architectural Historians, he is coauthor of *The Architecture of Frank Furness* and editor of *H. H. Richardson and His Office: Selected Drawings*.

Richard Oliver was an architect in New York and author of *Bertram Grosvenor Goodhue* and coauthor of *Architectural Drawing: The Art and the Process* and *America's Grand Resort Hotels*. He had previously served as curator of contemporary architecture and design at the Cooper-Hewitt Museum. He died in April 1985.

Peter C. Papademetriou, AIA, is associate professor of architecture at Rice University, Houston. A regular contributor to several architectural journals, he is currently researching the life and career of Eero Saarinen as well as the architecture and urban development of Houston, where he is also a practicing architect.

Selma Rattner is adjunct professor at the School of Architecture and Planning at Columbia University, New York, and teaches at the New York School of Interior Design. She is working on a biography of James Renwick, to be published by the Smithsonian Institution Press. A vice president of the Victorian Society in America, she lives in Kings Point, N.Y.

Laura Wood Roper became interested in Frederick Law Olmsted 40 years ago. Her articles on him in the 1950s represented the first research on Olmsted in a generation and sparked a revival of interest in his career. She is author of *FLO: A Biography of Frederick Law Olmsted*.

Leland M. Roth is associate professor of art history in the School of Architecture and the Allied Arts, University of Oregon, Eugene. He wrote his 1973 doctoral dissertation at Yale University on the urban architecture of McKim, Mead and White and has written *McKim, Mead and White, Architects* and several articles on the firm's work.

Nancy Halverson Schless is principal investigator for the William Strickland exhibition to be held at The Athenaeum of Philadelphia. A former director of the Society of Architectural Historians, she is contributing author of *Architecture in Wood* and a contributor to *Late Nineteenth Century Art,* as well as architectural journals.

David Spaeth is professor of architecture at the University of Kentucky, Lexington, and also maintains a private architectural practice. He is author of *Mies van der Rohe.*

Paul E. Sprague is professor of architectural history at the University of Wisconsin-Milwaukee. His writings on the Prairie School of architecture include two books—*The Drawings of Louis Henry Sullivan* and *A Guide to Frank Lloyd Wright and the Prairie School in Oak Park.*

Phoebe Stanton is a consultant on architectural design and previously taught art history at the Johns Hopkins University, Baltimore. She is author of *The Gothic Revival in American Church Architecture* and a contributor to *The Houses of Parliament* and has written on architecture for various journals.

George B. Tatum, Hon. AIA, was for 10 years professor of art history at the University of Delaware. A past president of the Society of Architectural Historians, he lives in Old Lyme, Conn., and continues to lecture and write on architectural history and landscape design. He is author of *Penn's Great Town* and *Philadelphia Georgian: The City House of Samuel Powel and Some of Its 18th-Century Neighbors.*

Theodore Turak is associate professor of art history at the American University, Washington, D.C., and has written and lectured on William Le Baron Jenney, the subject of his doctoral dissertation.

Further Reading

General Sources

Avery Obituary Index of Architects and Artists. Boston: G. K. Hall, 1963.

Committee for the Preservation of Architectural Records. *Directory of Historic American Architectural Firms.* Washington, D.C.: American Institute of Architects Foundation and Committee for the Preservation of Architectural Records, 1979.

Cook, John W., and Heinrich Klotz. *Conversations with Architects.* New York: Praeger, 1973.

Gebhard, David, and Deborah Nevins. *Two Hundred Years of American Architectural Drawings.* New York: Whitney Library of Design, 1977.

Jordy, William H. *American Buildings and Their Architects.* Vol. 3, *Progressive and Academic Ideals at the Turn of the Twentieth Century.* 1972. Vol. 4, *The Impact of European Modernism in the Mid-Twentieth Century.* 1972. Garden City, N.Y.: Doubleday.

Kostof, Spiro, ed. *The Architect: Chapters in the History of the Profession.* New York: Oxford University Press, 1976.

Lewis, Roger K. *Architect? A Candid Guide to the Profession.* Cambridge, Mass.: MIT Press, 1985.

Nevins, Deborah, and Robert A. M. Stern. *The Architect's Eye: American Architectural Drawings from 1799–1978.* New York: Pantheon, 1978.

O'Neal, William B., ed. *American Association of Architectural Bibliographers' Papers.* Vols. 1–11. Charlottesville: University Press of Virginia, 1965–75. Vols.

12–13. New York: Garland, 1977–79.

Pierson, William H., Jr. *American Buildings and Their Architects.* Vol. 1, *The Colonial and Neoclassical Styles.* 1970. Vol. 2A, *Technology and the Picturesque: The Corporate and the Early Gothic Styles.* 1978. Garden City, N.Y.: Doubleday.

Placzek, Adolf K., ed. *Macmillan Encyclopedia of Architects.* New York: Macmillan, 1982.

Richards, James M., ed. *Who's Who in Architecture: From 1400 to the Present.* New York: Holt, Rinehart and Winston, 1977.

Thorndike, Joseph J., Jr., ed. *Three Centuries of Notable American Architects.* New York: American Heritage, 1981.

White, Norval. *The Architecture Book.* New York: Knopf, 1976.

Wilson, Richard Guy. *The AIA Gold Medal.* New York: McGraw-Hill, 1984.

Withey, Henry F., and Elsie Rathbun Withey. *Biographical Dictionary of American Architects (Deceased).* 1956. Reprint. Los Angeles: Hennessey and Ingalls, 1970.

Wodehouse, Lawrence, ed. *American Architects.* Vol. 1, *From the Civil War to the First World War.* 1976. Vol. 2, *From the First World War to the Present.* 1977. Art and Architecture Information Guide Series. Detroit: Gale Research.

Adler and Sullivan

Morrison, Hugh. *Louis Sullivan: Prophet of Modern Architecture.* 1935. Reprint. New York: W. W. Norton, 1962.

Sprague, Paul E. *The Drawings of Louis Henry Sullivan: A Catalogue of the Frank Lloyd Wright Collection at the Avery Architectural Library.* Princeton: Princeton University Press, 1979.

Sullivan, Louis H. *Autobiography of an Idea.* 1924. Reprint. New York: Dover, 1956.

_____. *Kindergarten Chats and Other Writings.* 1947. Reprint. New York: Dover, 1979.

Charles Bulfinch

Kirker, Harold. *The Architecture of Charles Bulfinch.* Cambridge, Mass.: Harvard University Press, 1969.

Kirker, Harold, and James Kirker. *Bulfinch's Boston, 1787–1817.* New York: Oxford University Press, 1964.

Burnham and Root

Hines, Thomas S. *Burnham of Chicago: Architect and Planner.* 1974. Chicago: University of Chicago Press, 1979.

Hoffmann, Donald. *The Architecture of John Wellborn Root.* Baltimore: Johns Hopkins University Press, 1973.

Hoffmann, Donald, ed. *The Meaning of Architecture: Buildings and Writings by John Wellborn Root.* New York: Horizon Press, 1967.

Moore, Charles. *Daniel H. Burnham: Architect, Planner of Cities.* 1921. Reprint. New York: Da Capo, 1968.

Cram and Goodhue

Oliver, Richard. *Bertram Grosvenor Goodhue.* Architectural History Foundation. Cambridge, Mass.: MIT Press, 1983.

Alexander J. Davis

Davies, Jane B. "Alexander J. Davis, Architect of Lyndhurst." *Historic Preservation,* March–April 1965.

Davis, Alexander J. *Rural Residences.* 1837. Reprint. New York: Da Capo, 1980.

Newton, Roger Hale. *Town and Davis, Architects: Pioneers in American Revivalist Architecture.* New York: Columbia University Press, 1942.

Andrew Jackson Downing

Downing, Andrew Jackson. *The Architecture of Country Houses.* 1850. Reprint. New introduction by George B. Tatum. New York: Da Capo, 1968.

_____. *Cottage Residences.* 1842. Reprint. Watkins Glen, N.Y.: American Life Foundation, 1967.

_____. *Rural Essays.* 1854. 2nd ed. Introduction by George B. Tatum. Reprint. New York: Da Capo, 1975.

_____. *A Treatise on the Theory and Practice of Landscape Gardening.* 1841. Reprint. New York: Funk, 1967.

Orson Squire Fowler

Blumenson, John J. G. "A Home for All: The Octagon in American Architecture." *Historic Preservation,* July–September 1973.

Fowler, Orson Squire. *The Octagon House: A Home for All.* 1848. Reprint. New York: Dover, 1973.

Schmidt, Carl F. *The Octagon Fad.* Scottsville, N.Y.: Author, 1958.

Schmidt, Carl F., and Philip Parr. *More About Octagons.* Scottsville, N.Y.: Authors, 1979.

Stern, Madeleine B. *Heads and Headlines: The Phrenological Fowlers.* Norman: University of Oklahoma Press, 1971.

Frank Furness

O'Gorman, James F., and George E. Thomas. *The Architecture of Frank Furness.* Philadelphia: Philadelphia Museum of Art, 1973.

Cass Gilbert

Murphy, Patricia. *Cass Gilbert: Minnesota Master Architect.* Minneapolis: University of Minnesota Gallery, 1980.

_____. "Minnesota's Architectural Favorite Son." *AIA Journal,* March 1981.

Irving J. Gill

Gebhard, David. "Irving Gill." In *California Design 1910.* 1974. Reprint. Salt Lake City: Peregrine Smith, 1980.

Kamerling, Bruce. *Irving Gill: The Artist as Architect.* San Diego: San Diego Historical Society, 1979.

McCoy, Esther. *Five California Architects.* 1960. New York: Holt, Rinehart and Winston, 1982.

Greene and Greene

Makinson, Randell L. *Greene and Greene: Architecture as a Fine Art.* Salt Lake City: Peregrine Smith, 1977.

————. *Greene and Greene: Furniture and Related Designs.* Salt Lake City: Peregrine Smith, 1979.

Walter Gropius

Fitch, James Marston. *Walter Gropius.* New York: Braziller, 1960.

John Haviland

Baigell, Matthew. "John Haviland in Philadelphia, 1818–26." *Journal of the Society of Architectural Historians,* October 1966.

Hamlin, Talbot F. *Greek Revival Architecture in America.* New York: Oxford University Press, 1944.

Johnston, Norman B. "John Haviland, Jailor to the World." *Journal of the Society of Architectural Historians,* May 1964.

Tatum, George B. *Penn's Great Town: 250 Years of Philadelphia Architecture Illustrated in Prints and Drawings.* Philadelphia: University of Pennsylvania Press, 1961.

Tatman, Sandra L., and Roger W. Moss. *Biographical Dictionary of Philadelphia Architects, 1700–1930.* Boston: G. K. Hall, 1985.

Richard Morris Hunt

Baker, Paul R. *Richard Morris Hunt.* Cambridge, Mass.: MIT Press, 1980.

Thomas Jefferson

Kimball, Fiske. *Thomas Jefferson, Architect.* 1916. Reprint. New York: Da Capo, 1968.

Nichols, Frederick D. *Thomas Jefferson's Architectural Drawings with Commentary and a Check List.* 5th ed. Charlottesville: University Press of Virginia, 1984.

Nichols, Frederick D., and Ralph E. Griswold. *Thomas Jefferson, Landscape Architect.* Charlottesville: University Press of Virginia, 1977.

William Le Baron Jenney

Condit, Carl W. *The Chicago School of Architecture: A History of Commercial and Public Building in the Chicago Area, 1875–1925.* Chicago: University of Chicago Press, 1964.

Turak, Theodore. "Jenney's Lesser Works: Prelude to the Prairie Style?" *Prairie School Review,* Third Quarter, 1970.

————. "Remembrances of the Home Insurance Building." *Journal of the Society of Architectural Historians,* March 1985.

————. "William Le Baron Jenney: Pioneer of Chicago's West Parks." *Inland Architect,* March 1981.

Philip Johnson

Miller, Nory. *Philip Johnson/ John Burgee: Architecture.* New York: Random House, 1979.

Philip Johnson: Writings. Commentary by Robert A. M. Stern. New York: Oxford University Press, 1979.

Louis I. Kahn

Giurgola, Romaldo, and Jaimini Mehta. *Louis I. Kahn.* Boulder, Colo.: Westview Press, 1975.

Lobell, John. *Between Silence and Light: Spirit in the Architecture of Louis I. Kahn.* Boulder, Colo.: Shambhala, 1979.

Scully, Vincent, Jr. *Louis I. Kahn.* New York: Braziller, 1962.

Tyng, Alexandra. *Beginnings: Louis I. Kahn's Philosophy of Architecture.* New York: Wiley, 1984.

Wurman, Richard S., and Eugene Feldman, eds. *The Notebooks and Drawings of Louis I. Kahn.* 2nd ed. Cambridge, Mass.: MIT Press, 1974.

Benjamin H. Latrobe

Carter, Edward C., ed. *The Journals of Benjamin Henry Latrobe, 1799–1820: From Philadelphia to New Orleans.* Ser. I, vol. 3. New Haven, Conn.: Yale University Press, 1981.

Hamlin, Talbot F. *Benjamin Henry Latrobe.* New York: Oxford University Press, 1955.

Horne, John C., and Lee W. Formwalt, eds. *The Correspondence and Miscellaneous Papers of Benjamin Henry Latrobe.* Ser. IV, vol. 1. New Haven, Conn.: Yale University Press, 1984.

Norton, Paul F. *Latrobe, Jefferson and the National Capitol.* New York: Garland, 1977.

Stapleton, Darwin H., ed. *The Engineering Drawings of Benjamin Henry Latrobe.* New Haven, Conn.: Yale University Press, 1980.

McKim, Mead and White

Roth, Leland M. *The Architecture of McKim, Mead and White, 1870–1920: A Building List.* New York: Garland, 1978.

_____. *McKim, Mead and White, Architects.* New York: Harper and Row, 1983.

Wilson, Richard Guy. *McKim, Mead and White, Architects.* New York: Rizzoli, 1983.

Bernard Maybeck

Cardwell, Kenneth. *Bernard Maybeck: Artisan, Architect, Artist.* Salt Lake City: Peregrine Smith, 1977.

Longstreth, Richard. *On the Edge of the World: Four Architects in San Francisco at the Turn of the Century.* Architectural History Foundation. Cambridge, Mass.: MIT Press, 1983.

Ludwig Mies van der Rohe

Blake, Peter. *The Master Builders: Le Corbusier, Mies van der Rohe, Frank Lloyd Wright.* New York: Knopf, 1960.

Blaser, Werner. *Mies van der Rohe: The Art of Structure.* 1964. Reprint. New York: Praeger, 1972.

Hilberseimer, Ludwig. *Mies van der Rohe.* Chicago: Paul Theobald, 1956.

Johnson, Philip C. *Mies van der Rohe.* Museum of Modern Art. 1947. Rev. ed. Boston: New York Graphic Society, 1979.

Spaeth, David. *Mies van der Rohe.* New York: Rizzoli, 1985.

Robert Mills

Gallagher, Helen Mar Pierce. *Robert Mills.* New York: Columbia University Press, 1935.

Waddell, Gene, and R. W. Liscombe. *Robert Mills's Courthouses and Jails.* Easley, S.C.: Southern Historical Press, 1982.

Addison Mizner

Curl, Donald W. *Mizner's Florida: American Resort Architecture.* Architectural History Foundation. Cambridge, Mass.: MIT Press, 1984.

Olendorf, William, and Robert Tolf. *Addison Mizner—Architect to the Affluent: A Sketchbook Raisonne of His Work.* Fort Lauderdale, Fla.: Gale Graphics, 1983.

Julia Morgan

Heyman, Therese, and John Beach. *Architectural Drawings by Julia Morgan: Beaux-Arts Assignments and Other Buildings.* Oakland, Calif.: Oakland Museum, 1976.

Longstreth, Richard. *Julia Morgan: Architect.* Berkeley, Calif.: Berkeley Architectural Heritage Association, 1977.

Riess, Suzanne, ed. *Julia Morgan Architectural History Project.* Berkeley, Calif.: Regional Oral History Office, Bancroft Library, University of California, 1976.

Torre, Susana, ed. *Women in American Architecture: A Historic and Contemporary Perspective.* New York: Whitney Library of Design, 1977.

Alfred B. Mullett

Lehman, Donald J. *Executive Office Building.* General Services Administration Historical Study No. 3. Washington, D.C.: Government Printing Office, 1970.

Wodehouse, Lawrence. "Alfred B. Mullett and His French Style Government Buildings." *Journal of the Society of Architectural Historians*, March 1972.

Richard Neutra

Drexler, Arthur, and Thomas S. Hines. *The Architecture of Richard Neutra from International Style to California Modern.* New York: Museum of Modern Art, 1982.

Hines, Thomas S. *Richard Neutra and the Search for Modern Architecture: A Biography and History.* New York: Oxford University Press, 1982.

McCoy, Esther. *Richard Neutra.* New York: Braziller, 1960.

Frederick Law Olmsted

Fein, Albert. *Frederick Law Olmsted and the American Environmental Tradition.* New York: Braziller, 1972.

McLaughlin, Charles Capen, and Charles E. Beveridge, eds. *The Papers of Frederick Law Olmsted.* Baltimore: Johns Hopkins University Press, 1977–83.

Roper, Laura Wood. *FLO: A Biography of Frederick Law Olmsted.* Baltimore: Johns Hopkins University Press, 1974.

Stevenson, Elizabeth. *Park Maker: A Life of Frederick Law Olmsted.* New York: Macmillan, 1977.

Sutton, S. B., ed. *Civilizing American Cities: A Selection of Frederick Law Olmsted's Writings on City Landscape.* Cambridge, Mass.: MIT Press, 1971.

Pattern Books

Gebhard, David, Harriet Von Breton and Robert Winter. *Samuel and Joseph Cather Newsom: Victorian Imagery in California, 1878–1908.* Santa Barbara: University of California, 1979.

Grow, Lawrence. *Classic Old House Plans: Three Centuries of American Domestic Architecture.* Pittstown, N. J.: Main Street Press, 1984.

Hitchcock, Henry-Russell. *American Architectural Books: A List of Books, Portfolios and Pamphlets on Architectural and Related Subjects.* 1946, 1962. Rev. ed. New York: Da Capo, 1976.

Lafever, Minard. *The Beauties of Modern Architecture.* 1835. 2nd ed. New York: Da Capo, 1968.

Landy, Jacob. *Architecture of Minard Lafever.* New York: Columbia University Press, 1970.

Palliser, Palliser and Company. *Palliser's Late Victorian Architecture.* 1878, 1887. Introduction by Michael A. Tomlan. Watkins Glen, N.Y.: American Life Foundation, 1980.

Park, Helen. *A List of Architectural Books Available in America Before the Revolution.* 1961. Rev. ed. Los Angeles: Hennessey and Ingalls, 1973.

Sloan, Samuel. *The Model Architect.* 1852. 2 vols. Reprint. New York: Da Capo, 1975.

Stevenson, Katherine Cole, and H. Ward Jandl. *Houses by Mail: A Guide to Houses from Sears, Roebuck.* Washington, D.C.: Preservation Press, 1986.

Upton, Dell. "Pattern Books and Professionalism: Aspects of the Transformation of Domestic Architecture in America, 1800–1860." *Winterthur Portfolio*, Summer–Autumn 1984.

The Works of Asher Benjamin. Vols. 1–7. Reprints. New York: Da Capo, 1973–74.

I. M. Pei

Blake, Peter. "I. M. Pei and Partners." *Architecture Plus*, February and March, 1973.

Diamonstein, Barbaralee. *American Architecture Now*. New York: Rizzoli, 1980.

James Renwick

Rattner, Selma. *James Renwick, Architect: The Innovative Traditionalist*. Washington, D.C.: Smithsonian Institution Press, 1987.

_____. "Renwick, Aspinwall and Owen." In *Long Island Country Houses and Their Architects, 1860–1940*. New York: W. W. Norton, 1986.

Henry Hobson Richardson

Hitchcock, Henry-Russell. *The Architecture of H. H. Richardson and His Times*. 1936. 2nd ed., rev. Cambridge, Mass.: MIT Press, 1966.

Ochsner, Jeffrey Karl. *H. H. Richardson: Complete Architectural Works*. Cambridge, Mass.: MIT Press, 1982.

O'Gorman, James F., ed. *H. H. Richardson and His Office: Selected Drawings*. Cambridge, Mass.: MIT Press, 1974.

Van Rensselaer, Mariana Griswold. *Henry Hobson Richardson and His Works*. 1888. Reprint. New York: Dover, 1969.

Eero Saarinen

Papademetriou, Peter C. *Eero Saarinen*. G. A. Architect Series. Tokyo: A.D.A. Edita, 1986.

Saarinen, Aline R., ed. *Eero Saarinen on His Work: A Selection of Buildings Dating from 1947 to 1964, with Statements by the Architect*. 1962. Rev. ed. New Haven, Conn.: Yale University Press, 1962.

Temko, Allan. *Eero Saarinen*. Makers of Contemporary Architecture Series. New York: Braziller, 1962.

Skidmore, Owings and Merrill

Bush-Brown, Albert. *Skidmore, Owings and Merrill: Architecture and Urbanism, 1973–1983*. New York: Van Nostrand Reinhold, 1984.

Danz, Ernst. *Architecture of Skidmore, Owings and Merrill, 1950–1962*. Introduction by Henry-Russell Hitchcock. New York: Praeger, 1963.

William Strickland

Gilchrist, Agnes Addison. *William Strickland, Architect and Engineer: 1788–1854*. 1950. Rev. ed. New York: Da Capo, 1969.

Mahoney, Nell Savage. "William Strickland and the Building of Tennessee's Capitol, 1845–1854." *Tennessee Historical Quarterly*, June 1945.

William Thornton

Brown, Glenn. *History of the United States Capitol*. 1900. Reprint. New York: Da Capo, 1970.

McCue, George. *The Octagon: Being an Account of a Famous House—Its Great Days, Decline, and Restoration*. Washington, D.C.: AIA Foundation, 1976.

Reiff, Daniel D. *Washington Architecture, 1791–1861: Problems in Development*. 2d ed. Washington, D.C.: U.S. Commission of Fine Arts, 1977.

Stearns, Elinor, and David N. Yerkes. *William Thornton: A Renaissance Man in the Federal City*. Washington, D.C.: AIA Foundation, 1976.

Richard Upjohn

Stanton, Phoebe. *The Gothic Revival and American Church Architecture*. Baltimore: Johns Hopkins University Press, 1968.

Upjohn, Everard M. *Richard Upjohn: Architect and Churchman*. 1939. Reprint. New York: Da Capo, 1968.

Upjohn, Richard. *Rural Architecture*. 1852. Reprint. New York: Da Capo, 1975.

Venturi, Rauch and Scott Brown

Doumato, Lamia. *Robert Charles Venturi: A Bibliography*. Monticello, Ill.: Vance Bibliographies, 1978.

Venturi, Robert. *Complexity and Contradiction in Architecture*. 1966. Rev. ed. New York: Museum of Modern Art, 1977.

———. "Diversity, Relevance and Representation in Historicism, or Plus ça Change . . . Plus a Plea for Pattern All Over Architecture . . . with a Postscript on My Mother's House." *Architectural Record*, June 1982.

Venturi, Robert, and Denise Scott Brown. *A View from the Campidoglio: Selected Essays 1953–1984*. Edited by Peter Arnell, Ted Bickford and Catherine Bergart. New York: Harper and Row, 1985.

Venturi, Robert, Denise Scott Brown and Steven Izenour. *Learning from Las Vegas*. 1972. Rev. ed. Cambridge, Mass.: MIT Press, 1977.

Thomas U. Walter

Ennis, Robert B. "Thomas U. Walter." *Nineteenth Century*, Autumn 1979.

Gilchrist, Agnes Addison. "Girard College: An Example of the Layman's Influence on Architecture." *Journal of the Society of Architectural Historians*, May 1957.

Frank Lloyd Wright

Brooks, H. Allen. *Frank Lloyd Wright and the Prairie School*. New York: Braziller, 1984.

———. *The Prairie School: Frank Lloyd Wright and His Midwest Contemporaries*. New York: W. W. Norton, 1972.

Brooks, H. Allen, ed. *Writings on Wright: Selected Comment on Frank Lloyd Wright*. Cambridge, Mass.: MIT Press, 1981.

Hanks, David A. *The Decorative Designs of Frank Lloyd Wright*. New York: Dutton, 1979.

Hitchcock, Henry-Russell. *In the Nature of Materials: The Buildings of Frank Lloyd Wright, 1887–1941*. 1942. Reprint. New York: Da Capo, 1973.

Manson, Grant C. *Frank Lloyd Wright to 1910*. New York: Reinhold, 1958.

Meehan, Patrick J. *Frank Lloyd Wright Archival Sources: A Research Guide to Collections and Manuscripts*. New York: Garland, 1983.

Scully, Vincent, Jr. *Frank Lloyd Wright*. New York: Braziller, 1960.

Storrer, William Allin. *The Architecture of Frank Lloyd Wright: A Complete Catalog*. 1974. 2nd ed. Cambridge, Mass.: MIT Press, 1982.

———. *The Architecture of Frank Lloyd Wright: A Guide to Extant Structures*. Columbia, S.C.: WAS Productions, 1979.

Sweeney, Robert L. *Frank Lloyd Wright: An Annotated Bibliography*. Los Angeles: Hennessey and Ingalls, 1978.

Twombly, Robert C. *Frank Lloyd Wright: His Life and His Architecture*. New York: Wiley, 1979.

Wright, Frank Lloyd. *An Autobiography*. 1943. Reprint. New York: Horizon Press, 1976.

———. *The Natural House*. New York: Horizon Press, 1954.

Information Sources

The following organizations and agencies can provide further information on architects, American architecture and the preservation of historic buildings. For archival and photograph collections on specific architects, consult the resources listed in Further Reading.

American Institute of Architects
1735 New York Avenue, N.W.
Washington, D.C. 20006

American Society of Civil
Engineers
345 East 47th Street
New York, N.Y. 10017

American Society of Landscape
Architects
4401 Connecticut Avenue, N.W.
Washington, D.C. 20008-2302

Avery Architectural and Fine
Arts Library
Columbia University
New York, N.Y. 10027

Cooperative Preservation of
Architectural Records
Prints and Photographs Division
Library of Congress
Washington, D.C. 20540

Frank Lloyd Wright Foundation
Taliesin West
Scottsdale, Ariz. 85261

Frank Lloyd Wright Home
and Studio Foundation
National Trust for Historic
Preservation
951 Chicago Avenue
Oak Park, Ill. 60302

Historic American
Buildings Survey
National Park Service
U.S. Department of the Interior
Washington, D.C. 20013–7127

National Building Museum
The Pension Building
440 G Street, N.W.
Washington, D.C. 20001

National Register of
Historic Places
National Park Service
U.S. Department of the Interior
Washington, D.C. 20013–7127

National Trust for Historic
Preservation
1785 Massachusetts Avenue, N.W.
Washington, D.C. 20036

Regional Offices

Northeast Regional Office
45 School Street
Boston, Mass. 02108

Mid-Atlantic Regional Office
6401 Germantown Avenue
Philadelphia, Pa. 19144

Southern Regional Office
456 King Street
Charleston, S.C. 29403

Midwest Regional Office
53 West Jackson Boulevard
Suite 1135
Chicago, Ill. 60604

Mountains/Plains Regional
Office
511 16th Street
Suite 700
Denver, Colo. 80202

Texas/New Mexico
Field Office
500 Main Street
Suite 606
Forth Worth, Tex. 76102

Western Regional Office
One Sutter Street
Suite 707
San Francisco, Calif. 94101

Society of Architectural
Historians
1232 Pine Street
Philadelphia, Pa. 19107-5944

Index of Architects